WALKING ON EGGSHELLS

WALKING ON

Eggshells

Navigating the Delicate Relationship
Between Adult Children and Their Parents

JANE ISAY

DOUBLEDAY

FLYING DOLPHIN PRESS

New York London Toronto Sydney Auckland

PUBLISHED BY DOUBLEDAY/FLYING DOLPHIN PRESS

Copyright © 2007 by Jane Isay

All Rights Reserved

Published in the United States by Doubleday/Flying Dolphin Press, an imprint
of The Doubleday Broadway Publishing Group, a division of Random House,
Inc., New York.
www.doubleday.com

DOUBLEDAY/FLYING DOLPHIN PRESS and its colophon are trademarks of
Random House, Inc.

Book design by Mauna Eichner

LIBRARY OF CONGRESS CATALOGING-IN-PUBLICATION DATA
Isay, Jane.
    Walking on eggshells : navigating the delicate relationship between adult
children and their parents / Jane Isay. —1st ed.
        p. cm.
    1. Parent and adult child. 2. Baby boom generation—Family relationships.
3. Adult children—Family relationships. I. Title.
    HQ755.86.I83 2006
    306.874—dc22
                            2006025378

ISBN 978-0-7679-2084-1

PRINTED IN THE UNITED STATES OF AMERICA

10 9 8 7 6 5 4 3 2 1

FIRST EDITION

To my grown children:
May you be as lucky with your kids as I am with mine.

CONTENTS

Introduction

This book began with a surprise and a discovery. The surprise came almost a decade ago at Thanksgiving. One of my grown sons pulled a small, and he thought loving, prank, which upset me. I called him on it. "I'm old enough to be your mother. You shouldn't tease me that way," I said. Weeks later, I was telling a close friend about the episode, and she confessed that her grown children—daughters—were pushing her around in a way that she did not appreciate. She could not figure out how to deal with them. "I didn't realize how much grown children can hurt your feelings," she said.

That was the surprise. We compared notes about how vulnerable we felt with our grown children, and how hard it was to communicate with these new adults. My friend said, "I'm so glad we had this talk. I thought I was the only one."

That was the discovery. I was not alone, and neither was my friend. I realized that this stage of parenting is upsetting and confusing to a lot of parents. I hadn't read anything about it, and nobody brought it up in conversation. People don't talk about a problem if they think they are the only ones who have it. And there's a reason why so many of us are experiencing this: In a way, we're parenting pioneers. We're the first generation to have raised our children so permissively; and when they became adults, we could not call on our own experience as grown children, because our parents had raised us so differently.

Most members of the baby-boom generation grew up in families where, as in the TV show, father (and mother) knew best. Our parents' generation lived through the Great Depression and two world wars. They had a clear sense of the dangers that surrounded them—and us. They had to control our every action and decision, and many of us resented this. We did not like it at all when they told us what to wear (pink top and orange pants? never), where to go to school, what they expected of us (in no uncertain terms), whom to marry, and the career choice we should make (girls were expected to teach for a couple of years and then marry a good provider). As their children, we were lucky to have grown up in a much safer and more stable time of peace and prosperity. We raised our children differently from the way our parents raised us—under the permissive gaze of Dr. Spock. We fed them when they were hungry, put up with their outlandish garb, tried not to push them around, and wondered if they would ever shape up. The very spirit of the times encouraged a freer interaction between parent and child, which we happily adopted, despite our concerns.

Through all of this, we were ambivalent about authority and conflicted about limit setting. If we yelled at our children more than we would have liked, we felt bad. If we struggled with the idea that whatever they wanted to express was fine, we told ourselves we were raising creative children. Discipline was not our strength. We might have wished to be more authoritarian, but we didn't want to repeat what we felt were our parents' mistakes. When we saw "perfect" children, we wondered what was wrong with our own parenting skills, or we secretly suspected child abuse. Nevertheless, despite our ambivalence about authority, we made it clear to the children that we were in charge.

Twenty years later, they're still our children, but suddenly they are adults, with their own lives, their own friends and lovers, their own careers and lifestyles, and their own values. Often their decisions are not what we would have chosen—for ourselves or for them. We're at a loss to communicate our reservations, worries, and concerns, not because we can't put these feelings into words, but because the response we get often isn't pretty.

It is as if we awakened on a new planet and everything was turned on its head. The independence we worked so hard to instill in our children now feels to us like disinterest, and strong-minded youngsters sometimes grow into thoughtless adults.

We wonder: How can we get them to be more mindful?

We worry: Do we take the risk of speaking freely to them? We are perplexed.

We benefit tremendously from the more informal relationship we have with our grown kids; it's what they used to call "discipline" that troubles us. We all have to figure out new ways to express what we think and what we want— without pushing them away. Since there's nobody we can turn to with our questions about how to deal with the men and women who call us Mom and Dad, we need to create our own emotional guidance system.

I have traveled all over this country and interviewed dozens of parents and dozens of grown children, nearly seventy-five people in all. I interviewed grown children between twenty-five and fifty-five and parents in their late forties to their middle seventies. I wanted to get a fix on those decades between the time the kids leave home and the time when we really need their help. People love to tell their stories, and listening carefully is an art. I spent four decades as a book editor, working with experts in psychology, and was persuaded that stories are the best teachers. As a parent of two grown sons, and as someone who listens carefully, I have found some important truths for both generations.

Listening to grown children talk about their parents, I learned how deeply they love us and how desperately they want us to grow and change as they do. They want to be close, but they are exquisitely sensitive to any perceived or real assault on their autonomy and boundaries. Only when they trust that we respect them as adults can they feel free to return to the family. I was surprised to find that many people in their twenties and thirties were eager to tell me how much they worry about their relationship with their parents and how much time they spend puzzling over how to stay close and still be independent.

Most grown children are full of love for and gratitude to their parents, even if they don't show it. They want to establish a new relationship, one of greater equality, in which the parents' anxiety is not so overwhelming, and in which their parents' judgment is eased. They will return to parents who once were abusive, if that behavior has changed; and they will do what they can to meet their parents' needs, even when they are overwhelmed. On the other hand, they are hypersensitive about boundaries and will keep secrets from us if we step over the line. Many young people told me how much they resent being given advice by their parents, and how the narrowing of eyes in judgment makes them run for cover. As adults, they have the power to distance themselves from their parents, and they use that power when they need to. They can no longer be forced to accede to parental authority, and they have the right, and in some sense the responsibility, to make their own decisions, even if they make mistakes in the process.

Some of the parents I spoke with taught me how hard we have to work to welcome our children home as full-grown adults, not as former kids. Many parents have made the effort to adopt a new tone of acceptance and respect. By listening more carefully, and silencing their inevitable judgments, parents start to see and hear their grown sons and daughters more clearly, and the very act of listening and responding breaks down some of the self-protective barriers their children have erected. It takes effort to build a new lifelong relationship, one that works for both generations, and this effort pays off.

The first decade when children are out of the house, when they are in their twenties and early thirties, is a frustrating time for parents because they expect their kids to act like adults, and they are repeatedly disappointed. The kids ask for advice and ignore it; they call for comfort and then get off the phone—fast. They come home as adults and deposit their dirty laundry on the living room floor. It's infuriating, but like kids at all stages of development, they are training us. This is a period when kids are teaching their parents how to separate from them. Since children make it clear that they do not appreciate advice, parents can learn to button their lips. Since men and women in their twenties and thirties are very busy making their own lives, parents can adapt themselves to no longer being at the center of their children's lives and bearing the heavy responsibility that entails. Parents are being trained during this decade to enjoy living on the periphery of their children's lives, and to begin to pay more attention to themselves. Grown children teach us how to give up power and to modify expectations. In return, they can be a lot of fun, and we can embark on the next stage of our own lives.

⚬

I didn't find one parent who enjoyed this process of separation. It is no easier being the parent to an adult child than it was raising children at any other stage of growth. But since adulthood lasts for decades, we have plenty of time to adjust and to get it right. This opportunity to keep growing and changing along with our children is a challenge, but it's not a bad thing. We can allow time to heal the old wounds, and we can let the years soften our harsh judgments.

Everywhere I went, I found the bonds between generations to be supple and strong, even when relationships were strained. Members of both generations described an eagerness to keep on trying to get close to each other. It takes love and humility to accept our own weaknesses and to come to terms with the failings of our children. Accepting our grown children makes it easier to accept our own failings. The same holds true for them: As they come to see us as people, warts and all, their own vision of themselves as loving adults gets stronger and stronger.

I view these years with grown children as a river wide and long as the Mississippi. We all must learn how to navigate the waters. I have tried to find out where the hidden shoals are, how to steer through the treacherous currents.

I have found some of what is hidden and what needs to be dredged. We all want to sail home with love, respect, and peace. The kind people who told me their stories and shared their wisdom can help to make it happen for all of us.

PART I

Happy Families Don't All Look Alike

1

WHERE HAVE ALL OUR
CHILDREN GONE?

It was 1965, and I was pregnant with my first child—very pregnant. We lived in a university town, and I was the only working wife among the group of psychiatry residents. The other women were homebound with small children, living on their husbands' minute salaries. We were participating in the Mommy Wars long before these had a name. The other wives were jealous of my job, my freedom, our relative wealth, and the orderliness of our lives. I made them tense. At the time, I didn't have much sympathy for them. Competitive cooks, they didn't appreciate the Chinese takeout I served them when I entertained. They had messy kitchens, and their children were not much cleaner. Perpetually frazzled and resentful, they talked exclusively about babies, or so it seemed to me. I came to realize how difficult their job was, but at the time, I didn't get it. I suspected that some of the wives were secretly enjoying the fact that I was now pregnant. The size of my belly meant that big changes were approaching—especially for me!

We were leaving a birthday dinner party Harriet had thrown for her husband. She stood at the head of the steep stairs of their graduate-student housing, two flights up in an old house. The baby was on her hip, the toddler asleep on the couch. Harriet was exhausted. Her unruly red hair had curled tightly from the effort of putting on this party. Her face was shiny with sweat. She had cooked to beat the band. Harriet had removed much of the furniture in their apartment to set up tables for forty people. She'd made bouillabaisse for us all, except for my husband, who disliked fish; it was filet mignon for him—all this on a resident's salary.

I carefully navigated the staircase as we headed home. Harriet stood at the landing. "Just you wait," she called. "You'll see. You won't have a chance to pee, much less take a bath. Your blue couch will be ruined in six months. Say good-bye to your clean house and your wonderful life." I wept in the car on the way home. My feelings were hurt and I understood that it wasn't a prediction; it was a curse.

~

Life as parents did, of course, wholly change our style of living, but not exactly as Harriet had predicted. Parenting small children is a nightmare and a delight. Eventually, you do get to pee and wash your hair, the furniture is re-covered or replaced, and you get used to sleeplessness. You learn to change and adjust as your children grow, which is the only way to survive those early parenting years.

Then, if you're lucky, time passes and you begin to en-joy a quiet winter hour before dawn. And in a split sec-ond, the kids are coming home long after you've gone to sleep, and they don't wake up until the middle of your day. When they graduate from college, when they start out in their careers, when they fall seriously in love, you think that the job is done and the challenges have been met. That just isn't so, as we have all lived long enough to know. When their children become adults, many parents en-counter a whole new world of anxiety, miscommunica-tion, disappointment, and distance.

The empty nest is the harbinger of this new stage, when the youngest child goes away to school and peace and quiet descend. Many people feel relief, but lingering feel-ings of loss and separation can wash over them. It gets too quiet. The house is too neat. People may nod when we say we're feeling blue, but we all feel the need to shrug these feelings off. This first passage is well documented. The local paper usually runs a piece around Thanksgiving weekend, describing how when a college freshman comes home for the first time, it's a new experience for parents to have a child who suddenly knows so much more than they do about the world, and every imaginable subject. Still, the returning hero savors the taste of home cooking and sometimes even sits around and relaxes, just like old times.

One friend, whose eldest child is starting college in the fall, sighed and said, "She'll never live at home again." Little does she know that for many years to come, vacations, holidays, and summers will be filled with the sound of her daughter's voice, with her clothing and her moods. Her school memorabilia will clutter her room—which had better stay her room—and her term papers will be stored in the house forever. Little does she know how lucky she is that her daughter is just going away to college.

It's the second passage out that we and our children don't know how to navigate. We lack the language, we have no rules, and, most important, we don't have the perspective that would help us enjoy this time. Having our kids leave home and go out on their own is for many parents the culmination of decades spent raising them. "We raised them to leave us," we say, consoling ourselves when we are feeling lonely. Some people worry that staying close to their children will make them overly dependent, and others don't want to repeat the demanding attitude of their own parents. If they place a second call on the same day, they feel guilty; if they don't, they feel sad. It's as if we are being told to keep a stiff upper lip, kiss the children on both cheeks, in the French style, shake them by the hand, and bid them farewell. Nobody can do that, nobody wants to, and nobody should.

Enter an imaginary Harriet, back at the top of the stairs:

"You think you're done? You think that they're always going to return your calls? When they don't need you anymore, do you think they will stop by to chat? What about their wives and husbands? You might not get along with them. Life as you know it is going to take a turn for the worse."

Welcome to the stage when many parents feel that they are walking on eggshells.

Of course we want our children to be independent, autonomous adults. Because parents of our generation raised our children with more freedom, we hesitate to tell them what to do. So we tell them that we are confident they will make good choices, and then we worry a lot. Some of us pray. We hope that our children will bring us their problems, their dilemmas, and their concerns, because we think we still have good advice they will want to hear.

Understanding intellectually that we are no longer at the center of our children's lives is one thing, but in our hearts our children are still primary.

So when things are not the way we dreamed, we blame ourselves, just as we always did. Women who once were certain that they were terrible mothers if breast-feeding was not working now feel that they have failed when a grown son loses a job or a daughter gets divorced. Fathers who religiously coached Little League for years blame themselves when a son cannot make up his mind about his choice of career. It makes us feel like fools when we wake up in the middle of the night worrying about a son or daughter, mainly because we think we are the only ones in this predicament.

Here's what I have found. If you are worried that your son, who is in his late thirties, still isn't married or that your daughter refuses to face the fact that her career is at a dead end, you are not alone. If your son is in his late twenties and still hasn't finished college, this is more common than you know. If your child has rejected your values, know that this is happening all around you. If after you have welcomed your son or daughter's choice of partner into the family, you still can't meet his or her high standards of comportment, join the crowd. Some parents cannot fathom where their children come off expecting major financial help. Others are miserable because their children won't accept money or become resentful if they do take it. Some parents miss their grown children terribly; others are trying to figure out how to get them out of the house.

On the other side of the generational divide stand our grown kids, looking for us, as we seek them. They are struggling to come to terms with their parents as people, flaws and all. When they are disappointed in us, they feel terrible. When they cause a blowup at home, they feel awful. They resent it when parents meddle and are distressed when parents try to fix everything ASAP. They become seriously annoyed or embarrassed by parents' behavior in public. When they feel they are being judged, they become even harsher judges. They know it hurts when they can't chat long enough on the phone; they feel bad, but they have a job to do and a life to lead—they're busy. They want to bridge the gap with their parents. But as much as they love us—and the young people I talked with expressed great depths of love—they struggle to get it right, just as we do. Signs that we are trying to listen to them and accept them fully are met with pleasure and often with a response that shows they are trying to see us for who we are, too.

As I listened to people's stories, I realized that parents and their grown children are playing a new version of an old childhood game, blindman's bluff. One person is blindfolded and then tries to catch one of the other players, all of whom try to keep out of that person's way. But now both generations are wearing blindfolds, as parents and their grown children stumble around trying to find one another.

There's no problem between the generations that is more loaded than money. It stands for love, judgment, and responsibility. It is also a symbolic torch passing from one generation to another. Grown children may still expect to get what they want, even as their parents understand that they will soon be the ones in need.

Great Expectations

One of my favorite family stories from childhood took place one night when my brother and I were small. We were sitting around the dinner table and one of us piped up with this: "Daddy, when you die, can I have your watch?" I remember the surprise on my father's face, and then his laughter. We were tiny, and he was young, and he had many years—and possibly many watches—to go before his death. I wouldn't have minded if my children had asked such a question when they were young, but I'm not so sure how well it would sit with me today. Melanie's story made me remember my father's watch.

Melanie is a great spirit, she entertains with verve, she laughs a lot, and at sixty-eight she hasn't lost the light in her eyes, which reminds her friends of the party girl she used to be. With a shake of her head, an entrancing smile, and a mahogany laugh, Melanie has flirted with heads of state and great artists. She drinks, she smokes, she cusses, and she has a great heart. A widow with three grown children, Melanie tells me about her troubles with Julia, the only professional of the three. Julia, a tiny woman with jet black hair and very fine features, is lively and smart and sings like an angel. Her spirit fills her wonderful

Brooklyn brownstone with laughter, and her three children glow with the love of their family. Julia practices public-interest law, and her husband heads the legal-aid office in their borough. Melanie's second child is a writer, although she just gets by doing this. She is divorced from an extremely rich dot-com entrepreneur, who is thoroughly ungenerous. The third child, a son, is a brilliant maverick, who lives in the Southwest, composes music, and is deeply spiritual. He's always low on cash.

Melanie's life is centered on her family. Her husband died more than a decade ago, and she has turned her energy and focus on the children and grandchildren. She recognizes that she should broaden the focus of her life but cannot seem to do that. She has turned from party girl into earth mother, a role she has embraced fully. Melanie has been dipping into the capital of her small inheritance to take care of herself—and her children. She calculates how many years she has left of Mike's money, and she figures it will last a decade. It is running out, and Melanie worries. Of course her children know this. All three are very close to their mother. Melanie has her daughters and their families over for Sunday dinner every week, she throws the grandchildren's "sweet sixteen" parties in her apartment, she takes one grandson to spring training every year, and she shops with his sister. They all share a summer rental in the country every year. They are as close-knit a family as you can get. When she visits her musician son, Melanie sleeps on a futon—and her bones send out distress messages.

A year or two ago, Julia and her husband were

refinancing their house to make some improvements, and she asked her mother for a loan of ten thousand dollars, to be repaid when the bank financing came through. Melanie was thrilled to be able to write out a check for the loan. Then the refinancing didn't go through and the improvements did, and Julia couldn't repay the money. She asked her mother to forgive the loan and make it a gift.

For Melanie, ten thousand dollars is a considerable part of a year's living expenses, and Melanie told her daughter she couldn't forgive the loan, since her finances were strained. Julia was upset. She threw in her mother's face that she had been awarded scholarships throughout college and hadn't cost her parents anything, while they had paid for her sister's college tuition. And what about her brother? He was always asking his mother for help, she knew. It wasn't fair, and it wasn't equitable. It bothered Melanie deeply that Julia didn't seem to be concerned that she was running out of money. After two days of total misery, Melanie relented. She couldn't bear her daughter's anger; their relationship is crucial to Melanie's well-being.

Melanie knows that her second daughter, who just gets by, would sacrifice everything for her, but that doesn't cure this situation. She doesn't want to have to take anything from her children. The question of money turns into the question of age, the future, and who will depend on whom. It is a painful subject, and it kills Melanie to deny her children anything.

Melanie has found out that her children keep accounts of what she gives each of them. Julia resents what they paid for her sister's college. Both daughters know to the penny how much she gives their brother. This is nuts, Melanie thinks. Before Mike died, they were generous with all the kids, and whatever their children wanted, they got. Mike made a fine living, and it seemed as if good times would go on forever. When Mike died suddenly in his late fifties, each of the children received a small nest egg (that's what helped buy Julia's Brooklyn brownstone back when they were affordable), and Melanie got what seemed then to be enough money to take care of her for the rest of her life. But what seemed to be a lot of money years ago is no longer sufficient. Of course, if she had more, Melanie would continue giving all her kids whatever they might ask for, but that is no longer possible. Melanie is an old socialist who lives by the maxim "to each according to her need." She is shocked by the force of her daughter's anger and by the fact that all her kids have been keeping these accounts.

The issue of money crossing generations is becoming more loaded these days, because our generation faces the prospect of living longer, and having less to live on. Our parents endured the Great Depression, and we remember their stories of privation. We were able to insulate ourselves from financial insecurity, growing up, as we did, in the boom postwar years. But as the economy changes, many people worry about their future—and the future of their children.

Melanie's story is about money, but it is also about the passage of responsibility from generation to generation. Melanie can picture a time when her children will have to bear the brunt of her care, and Julia seems to be the most likely candidate for that job. Julia is not ready to consider that; she is still the daughter, in a family where the children come first. Last week, Julia announced that they were planning to fix up the basement. Melanie's heart froze.

~~~

Months later, I asked Melanie how things were going. Julia and her husband could no longer afford the private school their kids were attending, and Melanie decided to cash in some of the bonds that Mike had left her, so that she could pay for their schooling. She worries about the future, but her less fortunate kids, the musician and the writer, remind Melanie that she has food on her table and shoes on her feet. That's all these idealistic people will ever want or need—and they think that should be enough for their mother. I ask Melanie what would happen if she brought her three children together to talk openly about her finances and her worries about the future. Part of her would like to hear "Mommy, we'll never ask you for anything ever again, and we'll take care of you."

But Melanie also wants to remain the earth mother, someone who can happily meet all her children's needs. This is a central part of her identity. She dreads becoming dependent on her kids—for anything. The prospect of a day when she can no longer prepare Sunday dinner for ten people, when she can no longer take care of herself, and when they will take care of her, terrifies her. Money traveling across generations is morphing into the aging issue before her eyes. As Melanie depletes her savings, she comes closer to the point when she will depend on her grown children to care for her. She is confident of their love, but she'd rather stay young and independent.

※

Mothers of sons face a complicated situation. If they are ever going to stay close to their sons, they are going to have to develop a good relationship with their daughters-in-law. Teresa, a mother of three sons, thought she was doing very well with her oldest son's fiancée, when she took the wrong turn on a run through the park.

Teresa Trips

Teresa is on the phone. She is in a bad spot. The worst-imaginable thing that can beset a mother of sons has happened to her.

"My son's fiancée hates me," she moans. It is crucial to have your son's fiancée like you. Otherwise, you are in peril of losing him and his future family. I am growing to hate mother-in-law jokes, because they set up the expectation that the son's mother will be a pain in the neck. Teresa liked her future daughter-in-law, and she never intended to cause a rift. In fact, she thinks the world of Jamie (or she did), and she was really looking forward to having a relationship with her that was more like mother and daughter than mother-in-law and daughter-in-law.

A small woman with jet black hair, who gives new

meaning to the concept of high energy, Teresa is beside herself. She has always been loving and warm and accepting to Jamie, her eldest son's fiancée, because she thinks she is terrific. She is smart, beautiful, and an excellent influence on her son. Zach has moved through life on his own schedule. It took him eight years to get through college, and afterward he wandered a bit. Then he became a sports person and was dedicated to long-distance running. He and Jamie met at a New York marathon one October, and they have been inseparable since. He has proposed, and although there is no ring and no date, their prospects are sunny. Jamie and Zach are partners in a fitness enterprise, and they are on the verge of success.

"I want my sons to find women who will make them happy," Teresa tells me. She believes that nothing changes a son's life more than having a woman whom he tries to live up to. She welcomed this beautiful and smart woman into the family with all her heart.

Last summer, Teresa and her sister traveled to New York to join the young couple in a 10K race through the park. Everybody was looking forward to it. For some reason, Teresa's sister does not care for Jamie. Teresa does not know why, but since her sister and Zach used to be close buddies, she suspects her sister may be a bit jealous of Jamie. Teresa herself is just grateful that Zach has found the love of his life and is settling down.

The race was a challenge for Teresa, who hadn't run so many miles in years. She was huffing and puffing her way through the park when Zach dropped back to talk to her. Chatting with your grown son while you are jogging hard is no mean feat, but she was completely shocked by what her son had to say. He was not happy with Jamie. They were having trouble, and he was unsure about how to sever the work partnership if they broke up.

"What are you going to do?" she asked.

"All the business is in my name."

Teresa wasn't asking about that, so she phrased the question differently. "You love this girl. How are you going to end this relationship?" There was no answer as Zach sped off, while Teresa concentrated on keeping up the pace. That was the conversation she remembers: Zach was dubious about the relationship, and Teresa encouraged him to work it out with Jamie. The race was over, the weekend concluded, and Teresa flew home.

When she got home, she was greeted with an E-mail from Zach, saying she had been overheard saying bad things about Jamie to her sister. This was unacceptable, he said. She was the woman he was going to marry. Teresa could tell she was in trouble. We know that the worst thing you can do with a child or a friend who is complaining about his loved one is to second his complaints. But Teresa had done no such thing.

So she wrote him back and said, "Zach, I really have no idea what you're talking about, but if Jamie thinks I owe her an apology, I'd like to hear it from her." Unfortunately, Jamie wrote Teresa an angry and detailed letter. The diatribe was as much on Zach's behalf as on her own.

"You just have to realize that I have the heart of your son, and I know what his life has been like. Living with you and the deceptions in your family has led him to substance abuse and lies. That is not going to be the way we live," she wrote.

All her efforts to support Zach and his romance evaporated. Teresa is brokenhearted to realize that Zach harbored all these unspoken gripes. She recognizes that the first step is to deal with him, not Jamie. But she is devastated. The mother of three sons, she always dreamed of being close to their wives; it was the only way she could gain a daughter. Now, that dream seems to be lost.

The ill-fated race took place in October, and then, a month later, Thanksgiving was approaching. Her heart sank. The kids were not expected to come home, but she waited by the phone. Was she going to hear from Zach? Well, she did, but the conversation was cool and stilted. She guesses that politeness is the first step toward reconciliation. But Teresa will never forget the letter. It sits under other documents in her desk drawer, drawing her to read and reread it. Once something is committed to paper, it is impossible to ignore. Even if she works things out with her son, which she is determined to do, there is still Jamie's letter. She does not know whether it can ever be expunged from her memory, and whether she will ever feel at ease with Jamie again. Teresa still thinks that Jamie is the best thing that ever happened to Zach, but she knows that if Zach found another woman to marry, she would never discuss their relationship while running through a park.

+◯+

One of the problems when your children are grown is that nothing is settled for good. Teresa believed that things were great with Zach and that she had done just fine with Jamie. She thought her firstborn and his beloved were all set. Instead, Teresa found that a total misunderstanding during a race could ruin a relationship. Teresa thinks this is unfair, and she is right. That's the devilish paradox of parenting grown children. You can have a wonderful conversation with a son and think the relationship is finally on the right track, only to find that the next time you speak, he has reverted to an angry teenager. A daughter who is filled with gratitude for your generosity one evening may be frustrated with you the next morning.

That is why we so often feel that we are walking on eggshells—or running on eggshells, in Teresa's case. Even though we know that it is a good idea to think twice before we blow up at a grown child or melt down with an in-law, we're only human. It is very hard to act on this good advice when a phone call awakens you from a nap or when you are frustrated by something that has just happened and you then wind up having a difficult conversation with one of your children.

Good relationships take concerted effort, self-control, and clarity. As we all know, what looks easy on the surface is often the product of years of hard work. I had the opportunity to watch some wonderful parents in action and to hear how they do it.

Sheila's story is a template for closeness and ease between the generations. Her life is full of pain and of strength, but it is her perspective that is the most interesting and helpful to parents of grown children.

She Had So Many Children, and She Did Know What to Do

"Keep your mouth shut and your door open."

I'm sitting in a white wicker chair on the porch of large, rambling house on the Rhode Island shore. Sheila has brought out a pitcher of iced tea. At seventy-eight, her lovely round face is beautiful to behold. The lines around her mouth bespeak much laughter and happiness—and fierce determination. Sheila comes from a good Catholic family, and she has seven grown children. Six of them live with their spouses and their children, within ten miles of this house, the home in which Sheila raised them. The seventh is getting married in this town next summer and will settle nearby with his new wife.

When the youngest was six months old (he is now forty-three), Sheila's husband died of a heart attack at the dinner table. Sheila ran his business for years and raised her whole clan herself. She never remarried. Wonderful pictures cover the walls of the house: pastel drawings of the children when they were toddlers, framed in gold with pink or light blue trim, line the staircase. Beach shots of young couples holding their infants fill the study walls. Then there are the pictures of all the grandchildren posed near the ocean; once there were five, then ten, and now there are sixteen of them. Kevin, her middle son, turns up with his tool kit to fix the porch door. Her daughter Sheila arrives with her little one in tow to show her the T-shirts they just bought at Sears. Sheila greets them, they accomplish what they came for, and they leave. It's a gracious set of interactions.

Sheila has an excellent relationship with her grown children.

"What's your secret?" I ask.

She sits forward in her chair and tells me, bobbing her head for emphasis: "Keep your mouth shut and your door open." She sits back. Easier said than done.

"How do you do it?"

"When they were small," she said, "I was at business all day, and the housekeeper and my mother minded them. There were so many of them, they all had chores. Mother taught them to load the dishwasher, and they just loved doing it. They took care of one another, too, and they got into the dickens in pairs."

Maybe it's because she was exhausted at the end of the day, or maybe it's because the maid and her mother had responsibility for the kids while she was at work, but Sheila does not remember getting angry with them. She worried, but she rarely yelled at them. They would fight among themselves more than they fought with her. Perhaps they respected her and understood what fortitude it took to raise them all single-handedly. As they got older, their problems got bigger—some drank too much; others had school problems. But even then, Sheila didn't nag. She somehow understood that you can't make a person stop drinking, or eating, and you can't force a child to love school, or be a good student. Only one of her children still has a drinking problem, and Sheila is waiting patiently for him to seek help—on his own.

She admits to having a favorite, her namesake, a sturdy, down-to-earth brunette who looks just like Sheila did in the family portrait that was painted shortly before her husband's death. Little Sheila has an eight-year-old daughter, and her name is Sheila, too. The three Sheilas are a triptych of broad smiles, intelligent eyes, and faces crowned by short-cropped auburn hair. I would put my life in the hands of any of them. They radiate comfort and stability.

Perhaps because of the tragedy of her husband's death, perhaps because of her warm and accepting mother, who really pitched in when Sheila needed it, she is accepting of her children and doesn't take their flaws personally. She seems to have found a way to appreciate each of them as a person, and she has made a place in her heart for all their spouses, even the ones she doesn't care for. Her heart breaks when they are in pain, and she makes herself available to them.

She tells me, "There's always one who needs my help. Who it is changes. So I never have the same problem to deal with, and that gives me patience." She has strong feelings about giving advice. "No, that doesn't help. Sometimes when they fight with one another, it's bad, but then a holiday rolls around, and they know they have to make up, because they are coming to my house for the dinner."

Sheila's basement is filled with children's furniture and board games. Thanksgiving, Christmas, and Easter are all celebrated around her table. Perhaps all her children and grandchildren learned how to be kind and gracious from Sheila and from her mother, on whom she relied all those years ago when she was widowed and had seven small children.

She is selling the house next year, and little Sheila is building an addition to her home, where her mother will live for the rest of her life. Sheila is sad about leaving the home her father built for her more than half a century ago, but she looks forward to living with her daughter.

"I only made one requirement for my space. I need my own front door." I looked puzzled. Sheila leaned forward and nodded her head: "If Sheila is fighting with one of her brothers or sisters, he or she can still walk through my door without any bother."

Sheila is a wise one, and she transformed her misfortunes into good lessons for her children. The fact that there are seven brothers and sisters may have diffused some of the panic and anxiety that trouble small families. Small families are more intense, because there are fewer eggs in the basket. If there are many children, everyone is constantly reminded how different people are. Big families accustom parents to being out of control much of the time, and inure them to chaos. Parents in large families have to accept the wide variations from child to child, and they are also a lot more tired.

Perhaps her sons and daughters appreciate the amazing job Sheila did, raising them after their father died, and perhaps that makes it easier for them to show their love for her. Or perhaps Sheila absorbs her wisdom from the ocean, its eternal motion a calming presence that helps her maintain her loving and accepting perspective. Nature can do that.

Sheila's serenity is marvelous, but it's not everybody's style. Some people are just naturally more emotional and intense, and they can't help running into conflict with their kids. Conflict with grown children is frightening. When our children were young, we usually won. But now that they are adults and no longer depend on us, disagreements and differences of opinion carry new risks for us. It comes as a shock to realize that the dynamics change when the playing field is even, and that we have to adjust to new rules of engagement. Many parents cannot bear having their grown children angry with them, and so they avoid conflict. Even minor disagreements may mean that a child will disappear for a while, which can cause unbearable anxiety. It is a revelation to learn how vulnerable we are to their moods and behavior.

Lizzie is the mother of two grown daughters and the grandmother of two more girls. A divorced artist who had a hard childhood, Lizzie early on sensed that she would have to exert a mighty effort to maintain strong ties with her daughters. They were always arguing in this family—and making up. Lizzie has learned to manage conflict, and she adapts to the changing situations of her kids. She jumped right in when her elder daughter got into trouble. But she knew when to step back and let her daughter be an adult.

The Mother Who Knew What She Didn't Know

Lizzie and I are lounging on the comfy couches in her living room. The view, like many in San Francisco, is magnificent, but you don't really look out the window when Lizzie is in the room. A charismatic, energetic woman in her late fifties, Lizzie is all motion. Her hands flap. Her body moves. Her hair bounces as she gesticulates while sitting cross-legged on the couch.

Lizzie is twice divorced and has two grown daughters and two grandchildren. When the daughters were still teenagers, Lizzie realized that she was going to have to work extra hard to stay connected with them. She has kept up that effort ever since, and it has paid off. It hasn't been easy. They are all intense, and both girls have run into real trouble.

Sandy, the elder daughter, is the "good" one. Unlike her younger sister, Sandy was neat, quiet, a good reader.

When the school called about this child, it was to complain that she was hiding out in the girl's bathroom so that she could read her books without interruption. Lizzie's smile shows that this daughter was her dream come true.

But when Sandy was in college, she got pregnant, just as Lizzie had done nineteen years before. It was a terrible shock. Lizzie was heartbroken that her daughter was following in her footsteps. She went to the doctor with Sandy, urging him to tell her daughter that she should have an abortion, so that "her life wouldn't be ruined." (Imagine how Sandy must have felt—she wouldn't be alive if her mother had done what she was telling Sandy to do.) The doctor refused to listen to Lizzie. Sandy wanted to have her baby, who now, at thirteen, is the love of Lizzie's life. Sandy married the father, who never impressed Lizzie. Then Sandy's marriage faced some trouble. Lizzie witnessed her son-in-law push her daughter to the ground in the middle of a parking lot.

If he's that out of control in public, she worried, who knows what's going on behind the scenes at home?

Lizzie shakes her head. "You know as much as I do; you've read as much as I have. She said, 'First time, only time,' and I knew that if there was one time, there would be another time."

Lizzie and her former husband harangued their daughter for weeks. Sandy's father even invited Sandy and the girls to move into his Palo Alto house—without the husband, of course. Her dad said he would find her a good job nearby. That sounded just right to Lizzie, but not to Sandy.

"Meanwhile, she was saying, 'Hey, one time, only time,' and she was making all these excuses for him. I was still going on everything I'd seen and read—once and you leave!"

Lizzie reminded her daughter how her father also used to get out of control, and warned her that such behavior doesn't stop. Sandy refused to leave her husband. It was a battle royal. Lizzie wanted to get her daughter out of an abusive marriage, and right away, but she could not make that happen, any more than she could force her daughter to have an abortion.

Then a tiny voice in Lizzie's head said, Here are her choices. She stays with a man that she says is okay but I see as potentially violent. Or she leaves him. She doesn't have any real occupation or career. She's one of these people who can do anything well, but she has no credentials to do anything. And she's going to have to support two children.

Lizzie knew the statistics on a husband providing child support: about zero. And she also understood that this man would mean well, but his father had not been present in his life, so it would be all too easy for him to pay no child support. And then he might remarry. He might never help with his kids again.

"She was going to be a single mother raising two children on very little or nothing. Didn't have her college degree because she'd helped put him through school and graduate school. Which would be easier? Which would be better for her? The kids wouldn't have a father if she left, and she'd be condemned to the life of a single mother. Or she could stay with this potential violence."

Lizzie gets up for a glass of water and stares out the window.

"You tell me. What's the better deal? So I pulled way back. I told her, 'You're right; I don't know what's better for you. This is your life and you're going to have to make this decision. I will support you either way.' "

It worked. Sandy's husband began to control his rage, with the help of anger-management classes, and he is a devoted father. They went to counseling and seem to have improved their relationship.

"Better than ever—both of them say that separately to me," Lizzie says.

Sandy was right, and so was her mother. Lizzie knows who deserves the credit.

"They did it; I didn't do anything. But I could have broken that marriage up."

"And you were about to," I say.

"I was trying. Suddenly, I realized, You don't know. So what the hell are you doing? I watched my former husband with his three kids. He thinks he knows what's best for them and he pays the way for them to do whatever he thinks is best for them. They don't have a relationship worth a nickel."

Harriet, my hostess in the sixties was right about one thing. Giving birth isn't the end of the process; it's just the beginning. It came as a shock, the morning after my first child was born, to realize that I had this person for life. Like all parents of young children, I counted the days until they could walk and talk, read, and go to school, get into college, and find their life's work and their life's partner. Each time, I thought my hard work would be over. I was wrong each time. Once my sons met each of these milestones, something new came up.

We have the choice of adjusting to each new set of challenges or not. Even if we don't really want to do this, we have a secret ally: the law of small changes, which says tiny differences can accomplish big things over time. Our grown kids notice and appreciate even minute differences in how we treat them. This will make them nicer. When their tone or mood improves, we feel better. And so it goes. Happily, there's plenty of time to make these tiny adjustments, and it's never too late.

Close friendships offer a good model for striking this new balance. We have been peers with our friends from the start. The boundaries are already in place. Since we didn't raise them, we don't feel the need to run their lives. We listen to them and we are careful about the advice we offer. We rely on friends, and we learn from them. We don't sniff at their taste in furniture or the messiness of their kitchens. We empathize with their pain, and we celebrate their joys. We encourage them, as they encourage us. Friends hold one another when they weep, and dance at their children's weddings. Friends have the great advantage of choosing one another, but they don't share the memories and experiences of living in close quarters for decades. Imagine having a relationship with our kids that is as easy as friendship and as close as family.

The men and women who call us Mom and Dad want that ease, too. They yearn for the end of conflict; they try to accept us warts and all, and they want genuine acceptance in return. Having flown the coop, they also are a bit lost and confused about how to find their way back home. But the love and gratitude are there, just around the corner, as you will see in the next chapter.

2

Hiding in Plain Sight

"I have one father, one mother, one brother, and one sister. They're it. If I don't value them and love them and expect the same in return, I just can't imagine having to go through every day," says a twenty-five-year-old man who chose to live a continent away from his parents.

"My mother always made me feel like I was unbelievably important and precious to her, and I carried that with me in my life. That's a great gift. She still drives me crazy, but I am learning to give that up, and now I appreciate what I do get, which is a hell of a lot. How many people can

say they always felt loved and valued? I don't know many,"
a successful artist, whose mother actively discouraged her
from following her dream, tells me.

"I am enormously grateful to her, because she is a very
strong woman and a very loving woman," I hear from a
daughter who trades hurtful messages with her demanding mother.

"Those ways of loving I have carried with me, and this
idea that family is first, and that love and family come before anything else—after God, of course, but before work
and money and everything else." I hear this from a woman
who has decided to settle thousands of miles away from her
parents.

I had expected to hear about the frustrations grown
children have with their parents, but it came as a happy
surprise that every conversation started with expressions
of love and gratitude. Along with the love and gratitude
that many men and women in their twenties, thirties, and
forties expressed, there are, of course, issues they have
with their parents. They are critical of their parents, concerned about the quality of their interactions, resentful of
errors their parents made when they were young, and hypersensitive about their parents' comments now. They
told me about the needs they wished their parents could
meet, and they described the trouble they have in expressing themselves directly to the older generation. Still, these
grown children began and ended our conversations with
expressions of gratitude, admiration, and love. The older
they are, the more aware they are of the problems we
faced. They come to understand that it takes work and pa-

tience to establish a peer relationship across the generations.

In the daily back-and-forth of busy lives, that love and
understanding is hard to see. The silences that upset us,
the distance we feel, the guilt we carry from the past, and
the disappointment that results from knowing we don't
have the kind of relationship we want with all our children—
these should be understood in the context of love, which is
a two-way street between generations. The great French
essayist Montaigne observed that a parent's love for a child
is wholly different from a child's love for a parent. He was
right about that.

We still love our children as if they were small, and we
struggle to accept them as they are now. They remember
the simple love they felt for us when they were young, but
that is no longer appropriate, because they don't want to
be under our control anymore. People who once imagined parents as all-powerful and perfect struggle to come
to terms with habits that irritate them. They are torn between that childhood closeness and the adult relationship
they want. It is only natural that they have difficulty in
finding that separate and equal stance. We do, too.

A young father in his thirties put it this way: "For a
parent to say a child is a friend implies you haven't formed
this child in your womb, that you haven't been there to kiss
his head when he hits it against the wall. For years, the
kid's hunger was your hunger; the kid's pain was actually
your pain. If you didn't have that sense of connection with
your child, you'd be inhuman. And then to go snip some
of these cords, it's hard. It seems so violent."

It isn't easy for parents to construe their grown children's behavior as loving when they are not returning our phone calls, when they criticize us, fight with us, and show a certain disdain. But most often the love is there—hiding in plain sight.

Many of them remember the hard time we often gave them, but gratitude still comes into play, gratitude for what we did for them. They have not forgotten our small sacrifices and daily kindnesses. They are also grateful for the gift of life. They appreciate much more than they tell us, and their voices don't always communicate their positive feelings. Grown children, especially those in their twenties and thirties, cannot afford to come back fully into the family—yet.

We just need to remember their expressions of resentment or anger don't equal lack of love. Being testy on the telephone or blowing up at the Thanksgiving table is not about love. Even berating us for having misspoken to a wife or an in-law doesn't signal lack of love. Anger because we can't or won't meet their needs doesn't make love go away, either. This should come as no surprise. After all, when we yelled at them, showed our disappointment, corrected their manners, and judged their friends, we did it out of love. As children they didn't see it that way, but as they get older, they may even understand our point of view, especially when they become parents.

This unspoken love and gratitude is often linked with forgiveness, which surfaces when parents change their old behavior. I learned this especially from sons and daughters of men who were abusive fathers. Once these fathers

stopped drinking and raging, and showed that they wanted
a loving relationship with their children, the grown kids I
spoke with were eager to take them back into their lives.
When mothers who seemed to their younger children to
be thoroughly self-involved became caring and beloved
grandmas, they were appreciated and adored for it.

Grown children told me about their frustrations and
hurts, their fears for the future, and admitted that they
had chosen to live far away in order to keep things on an
even keel. Daughters spoke about mothers who seemed to
need to be mothered by them. Others described the cur-
tain of silence that falls the minute they hear anxiety and
panic in their parents' voices when they tell them their
worries or problems.

Diane's relationship with her mother and her father offers a view of love that persists with one easy parent and
one difficult parent. I have only sons, and my mother and
I were not close, so I never experienced that special something between a mother and daughter. When women told
me that they were best friends with their daughters, I
smiled and thought, I'll believe it when I see it. Then I
saw it.

Best Friends

"My dad has told me that when he looks at me, he sees the baby with the pin curls. That's not how my mother saw me; I think she saw me as a person who she really liked, who she had the great luck of having as a daughter."

Without intending to, Diane articulates a checklist of what grown children want: no unsolicited advice, no pushing for change, no judgment, respect for boundaries, an attitude of genuine love and acceptance. This is a high standard for ordinary mortals, but listen to this daughter's sense of her mother's love.

"Mom was much less of the kind of person who would give you unsolicited advice, or always tell you how to change your life, or passing judgment in some way. She was somebody who made me feel good about myself." She seemed to be able to achieve the "friend" status without breaching Diane's boundaries, or her own.

"My relationship with my mom, barring the teenage years, was always incredibly easy, incredibly warm. From very early on, she seemed to have a knack for being a parent and a friend at the same time. She was always my mom, but she was really as much a friend as anything else."

It was clear that they could be girlfriends and spend unlimited amounts of time together.

"We had a house up in the mountains, and Mom and I would take these really long walks. We'd go around the lake and up the back trails to the top of the mountain, and then cut over the ridge and drop down to the house. It was one huge loop. I remember Mom confided in me afterward, saying that Dad's reaction was, 'What did you find to talk about that whole time?' So for Dad, it doesn't come naturally. For my mom, what did we find to talk about? Men, movies, finance, politics, teaching, everything—the way you do with a girlfriend. When you're with somebody really close, in three hours you basically fix the entire world—and notice the wildflowers in the process."

Diane's family followed her father's jobs all over the world; her mother was the anchor. Diane's mom took over when her husband was away, and she cushioned the blows of their peripatetic life. She was a magnificent person. I had heard about Diane's mother from other people who had validated her description.

Then Diane's mother developed a terrible form of cancer and spent her last years fighting for her life. Diane moved home to help her, and she spent a lot of time with her mom in the hospital.

"I'd essentially move her as far as I could to the edge of the hospital bed and I would climb on, and we'd just sit there together and hold hands, either watch a movie or not. It made me feel totally peaceful, and you could tell she was. 'Ah, this is good,' she'd say. I can't imagine ever doing that with my dad: different personality, different relationship."

Diane and her father are still grieving for that wonderful woman. Diane decided to settle in their hometown, so she spends a lot of time with her father now that he has retired and is alone. She is gradually improving her relationship with him, but there is still work to do.

Diane's description of her father provides a list of some of the things that put our children off: being judgmental, being critical (especially for women when it comes to their appearance), not making them feel known and understood, being easily distracted. Diane's dad is a handsome charmer in his early seventies, a man who isn't so easy to be around. He always was judgmental.

"I would come home from school and make a sandwich, and I remember he would give me the look. It's the same look he gives when somebody takes a third drink at a party. He was the kind of person who, fast-forward several years, would never just say, 'Gee, you look great.' It was always, 'Gee, you look great. You look so much better.' "

Diane adopted her father's judgments of herself, as children tend to do. What she heard was that she had been looking like shit.

It took her years to get up the courage to say, "You know, Dad, when you say that, all I hear is that you feel I've been looking terrible. That's all I hear. I don't hear the compliment in that." He has not spoken that way since. Diane is gradually getting through to him, but it's not easy. Diane used to take her father's perennial distractedness personally: If he lost focus, she felt she must not be interesting. But now she has discovered that when she tells him what she feels, things improve.

"It's not like we had a bad relationship. It's just there was a distancing."

Diane is making that chilling point about what we risk when we don't pay careful attention. When they are adults, our children possess the ultimate weapon: distancing. In order to keep from feeling hurt and put down, they just recede from us and get on with their lives. They will be in touch when they feel they must (calls from the cell phone driving to work); they will appear on family occasions, but they will never take an easy stroll with us through the hills or in town. That is the emotional dimension of distancing. There is another strategy, putting physical distance between the generations. It is a well-known recipe for keeping peace in the family. Many people must live far from their parents because of work or marriage, but grown children who feel the need or the desire to be close often try to find a way to get closer to home. A son might make it clear to his boss that a transfer would be a godsend; a daughter might make her choice of her job based on proximity to the family. Others come home whenever they can—and many parents gladly pay the airfare, even though their grown kids are old enough to pay it for themselves. Tickets home seem to have a special meaning to both generations.

Diane chose to live near her father, and their relationship has improved. He calls her to ask how to get a spot out of his sweater or to how to cook a chicken. He sometimes calls seven or even ten times a day. Oh please, get a girlfriend! Diane thinks. Then he started really confiding in her about his relationship with his girlfriend, which is something she doesn't much care for.

"I know way more about their relationship than I feel comfortable with. But he doesn't have the good guy friend he could do that with. Because he respects my opinion, I was the one he would turn to. I would say, 'Okay, enough,' and try to put up some boundaries, but he's not the greatest guy on boundaries."

She is glad to put up with him, though, because he's her father, and she loves him, despite all their issues. While she is working things out with her father, Diane, who never married, ponders what might have been if her mother had been the one to survive, not her father.

"We'd probably be looking at a very different scenario. She and I probably would have bought a house together. I can't imagine doing that with my dad. Dad must be aware of the difference in the relationships, and I'm sure it's a little bit painful for him."

Perhaps Diane's father was content to let his wife do the relating to the children and, because of that, didn't have to face the consequences of his behavior. Diane has taken on her mother's role as teacher, and her father is turning into a good student. Diane and her father are experiencing gradual change, in increments so small that they are difficult to notice. Diane believes that all this is happening because of her mother's influence.

"Maybe Mom's energy is infusing him and sort of steering him. Or the memory of the kind of relationship she did have with us, when he did not, makes him want to turn himself around."

Diane's view of herself and her father changes as both give up the stance of judgment. Knowledge about how to form a relationship may be her mother's greatest legacy.

Our kids watched us like hawks when they were small, and they still bear our stamp, because we were their first teachers. Years later, we may be able to catch a glimpse of the rudimentary lessons we taught them—in their mannerisms, their behavior, and their tastes. Sometimes when we visit, we are amateur archaeologists, scoping out the traces of how we raised them in the way they live now. Is their taste like ours? Is their home peaceful or noisy, neat or messy? Even if we find evidence of the past, history is nothing when compared to the present. The sins of yesterday are forgiven if today is pleasant, and the gifts of the past are dimmed if today is difficult. This is good news and bad news.

The good news is that our children are still exquisitely sensitive to us. I have been amazed by how little it takes to begin to break down the barriers between parent and child. It surprised me to see how many grown children forgive their parents for behavior that was unacceptable when they were children.

The bad news is that we do have to stop treating them like children, and both generations need to move beyond the past. So, a mother who raised her children alone, having saved them from an abusive father, cannot expect her children to meet her every need when they are grown. They are grateful, but they have lives to lead. And a father who sacrificed for his son can't hold those early years over the grown man forever. We have to change how we see them and how we treat them. That means we have to keep on growing and changing.

More good news: Small changes in our behavior can make a big difference in our relationships. There is no formula for change, but, in fact, we are the best experts on what we do that makes them nuts or hurts their feelings. If we want to, we can improve the situation. You can catch sight of the clues that things are improving: they are easier in our company, they are more relaxed in conversations, and they begin to reestablish old habits of closeness, and they are more mindful of our needs. They might even call up just to say hello.

Erin's father is reaping the rewards of his changed behavior. He has his daughter back. For much of her life, Erin did not think she could bear to spend time with him ever again.

Childhood's End

"A person who is alcoholic and manic-depressive can be very mean. It's very hard to differentiate between who the person is, essentially, and what that behavior means. Are you essentially a good person who is sick? Or are you just a mean bastard?"

These are the questions that Erin asked herself for the decades when she did not see her father, and didn't care to. A therapist who was trained in a humanistic tradition, he was a drunken, angry man, and a cheating husband. Her mother went to school and worked to support this tall, well-spoken healer, but she failed to notice the signs of his illness and cruelty. People then didn't understand bipolar illness or how to treat it. He played favorites among the siblings; he had affairs with patients, and squandered his tiny salary on the ladies. One Sunday night, her mother scooped Erin and her sisters out of their beds and into the car, drove off to pick up her son at an assigned meeting place, and moved them all into the home of an old friend. Her brother lived with his father for a year after they fled, but Erin was done with this man. He never hit Erin, but she saw him slap her mother on the night she left—at the end of the long Thanksgiving weekend. Erin had no time for this man. He didn't attend her high school or college graduations, they rarely spoke, and her brother walked her down the aisle when she married. She did run into him once, at a family occasion, and he spoke so cruelly about her husband that the memory of this encounter still makes Erin flush.

Estrangement from her father was a fact of Erin's life.

She kept up a relationship with her paternal grandmother, though, and she loved this woman dearly. Naturally, Erin attended her grandmother's funeral, where she once again encountered her father.

"You know, it was age, medication, a number of other things, and he wasn't drinking. He had softened tremendously, so for whatever reason, I thought I'd like him to know my children."

He has turned into a wonderful grandfather. Erin and her family visit with him and his wife regularly. Like many reformed abusers, he now makes every effort to be agreeable. Because he changed his behavior, Erin started rethinking her view of him. She understands the role of effective medication, which was not available years ago, and she can also begin to rediscover the good man who is her father.

In some ways, their relationship is relaxed and fun now, because it is very straightforward. Father and daughter always enjoyed books, and now they can go on for hours about what they are reading. They know exactly what to expect from each other.

"We don't talk about the past at all. I feel like that man has been through so much pain in his life, and I think he's done very bad things, and I no longer wish to judge him for it. I just don't."

And her father has done his best to connect with her husband, about whom he was once so cruel.

"He worked so hard to make up for that. He endlessly said wonderful things about what a wonderful father he is and so on. Luckily, I have a very forgiving husband, and I'm very lucky in that regard."

So there it is, forgiveness and a determination to reconnect. Her father has changed, and Erin's needs have changed. She doesn't ask for a profound relationship; she just wants an easy one.

Her father plays the role of loving grandfather, largely because he is intent on getting his daughter and her family back. Hiding in plain sight for Erin and her dad are their shared past and the years of estrangement. The contrast between then and now somehow makes their ease together feel sweeter. She had long ago given up expecting much from her father, so every good meeting is a gift.

Mother's Not-So-Little Helper

"I'm not your mom. Can't you just be my mom?"
"I've been bitten by dogs before—you know, you reach out with love and they bite you? That's how I felt: totally betrayed."

Parents who don't get along with their children begin to think that they aren't loved. They are plagued with guilt about the things they didn't do. They know that honest expressions of their own anger will get them into more trouble with their kids, and they cannot find the language to begin a genuine conversation about the past and the present. Some parents become hopeless and withdraw, just as their children do. Distance is a two-way street. This is something Dolores discovered when she became stuck in a cycle of anger and silence with her eldest daughter. They were at loggerheads for years, and it seemed hopeless to both of them.

World history played a role in Dolores's plight. She is a survivor of World War II. Her mother brought her to America from the Philippines when she was a baby. Mother and daughter narrowly escaped the Japanese. Her father was not so lucky. He spent the war years in a Japanese concentration camp. Dolores's mother witnessed her own mother being beheaded as a spy. It left a terrible scar on this woman, who had been raised in a prestigious and wealthy family and came to America without money and status. She and her husband reconnected after the war, but the damage was too severe, and their marriage was not happy. For Dolores's mother, life was a series of losses from which she never recovered. Both of Dolores's parents died when she was in her twenties, so she had to invent herself as a loving mother, and then she had to reinvent herself as a good grandmother.

Dolores lounges in the sunroom, a lanky, lovely woman who clinks every time she moves. She's dressed western-style, in denim and embroidery, and wears lots of jewelry. Her gray hair is cut in a bob, and I could swear she's wearing moccasins—she has the air of an Indian princess. Dolores loves the West, and she dresses accordingly. She tells me that her two daughters are goddesses, but their relationship with her hasn't always been easy. Things almost fell apart with Vanessa, the eldest, around the time that Vanessa had her first child. Both daughters were grown and out of the house by then.

"I couldn't imagine life without my daughters. I thought it would be a very empty space, because they were so important to me, but then when they left, I managed to fill up the time very well—in fact, too well. And the issue I had with Vanessa was that she really wanted me to be like a grandmother—you know, not hover, but make cookies, be around, help." This didn't register with Dolores. Here's how the troubles began.

"This is the big blowout we had. It started when she was pregnant with her first baby, and she had morning sickness. We live on a farm, and things don't smell pristine on a farm. We have animals. We have goats; we have chickens. She was throwing up every morning, but I didn't know about it. I try to clean, but I am not a very good cleaner, and there was some dust in her room. She was just a bitch. She complained. She criticized me. Nothing would please her. She accused me of losing something that later I found, and she never thanked me for it. I was really hurt. We tried to work it out during that visit. I mean, I loved her so much and wanted her to be happy."

But Dolores was angry with her daughter, very angry.

"I really felt like cutting off from her. It hurt so much.

"She'd come downstairs and say, 'God, I can't stand being in this house! It's so awful and dirty.' It wasn't. I'd spent a long time cleaning it. It was just like my mother again."

"Your mother was like that?" I ask.

"My mother always made us do the cleaning."

Dolores resented this as a child, and Vanessa's tone set her off terribly—she felt as if she were hearing her mother's voice again. Growing up in her sad family, Dolores and her sister were forced to clean her mother's house, and when they were sent to the grandparents, they were treated like scullery maids. Dolores's parents both died young, and by the time Dolores married and had children, nobody was alive to help her learn how to parent. Now she feels she was a pioneer, teaching herself how to be a grandmother.

"The only model I had, my own mother, lasted until I was twenty, and we were not on good terms when my parents died, so this has been a life journey for me, trying to find the right way to have a relationship with my adult daughters."

The fight with Vanessa was just the beginning. Dolores was hurt and angry, and she even thought about breaking off the relationship. In addition, her life as a musician was picking up.

"When the baby was due, I was in a musical, and I told her I couldn't be there for the birth. She had a fit. She was so angry with me that I got out of one week of rehearsals and did go. I actually arrived there the night the baby was born and was there for ten days. But the fact that I had said I couldn't be there really hurt her. She was so mad."

Dolores's face darkens when she remembers this time, and her pale blue eyes look even larger than before.

"I know; it's my fault. We never did anger well in my family."

One of the easiest things to do, in the face of a grown child's rage, is to withdraw. Dolores threw herself into her music.

"I didn't deny her my presence because I was angry, but it was easy for me to make other plans, to say, 'Well, she doesn't care about me; I'll do the other stuff.' And how would I know that she cared about me? I never had anybody take care of me when I was raising my kids. You know, we try to do our best, but sometimes we struggle."

Dolores and Vanessa were losing each other.

"When we were talking and trying to get through this awful fight, I said, 'Vanessa, what I feel is the criticism from you, just like my mother would do to me.' "

Dolores kept hearing her mother's voice in her daughter's words, and she was reacting like the child, not like the mom.

Vanessa certainly got that. "Can't you see me not as your mom but as your daughter and just be a good mom to me?" she asked her mother. It didn't get better when Vanessa had her second child.

"I was there, but I left the next day, because I'd been there a whole week. I had a wedding to play in. Music is very important to me, and now that I don't have kids, I have an opportunity to get into it."

The choice for Dolores was easy: a miserable, tense time with an angry, unforgiving daughter and her babies, or a gig where her friends and audience appreciated her.

Dolores had not experienced the back-and-forth within a strong family of adults. She had not lived through the fights and the reconciliations that grown children have with their parents. She had done it all alone, and so could Vanessa, she felt. It took the intervention of her younger daughter, Alison, to bring them back together.

Alison told her how furious Vanessa had been when her second child was born and Dolores departed the scene. So after Vanessa's third child was born, Dolores went to take care of them, thinking that she could make it up to Vanessa. But then they had another horrible fight. Dolores wanted to leave on the spot, but she didn't; she somehow lasted through the visit, but she despaired of her relationship with her elder daughter. Again, Alison stepped in to make peace between her mother and her sister.

"When I would fight with Vanessa, Vanessa would call Alison, and then Alison would call me and say, 'Look, Mom, it's just a misunderstanding. Go talk to her.' "

Over time, it worked out. After that last traumatic visit, Dolores came home and thought things over.

"I took total responsibility for that fight, even though I wanted to blame her for it. I thought about what it was in me that attracts the bad part of Vanessa, when there is so much good in her. I must be vibrating anger at her; I must be giving her negativity. I reached into my heart, and I thought, Okay, I have not let this thing go about when she was pregnant and was so horrible."

So she wrote her a long E-mail, saying, "Vanessa, I've really been thinking about this and I want to take responsibility for my part in it. I've been carrying around anger at you from the time you were first pregnant and didn't ever tell you. So when you've met me, you've been feeling it and so you've reacted to it, but we've never had a chance to talk about it."

Dolores's apology had an astonishing effect. Vanessa was relieved of her anger and accompanying guilt; soon their relationship became a little more normal. Dolores was delighted when Vanessa actually inquired about her day. Dolores only needed a little more coaching from Alison.

"I'm kind of telephone-phobic. I don't like to call, but Alison told me how important it was that I call Vanessa and not just send her E-mails. I started calling her more."

Once things got on track, Dolores sensed love instead of criticism and anger from her daughter. She needed that. It helped her deepen the connection, and she stopped dreading her conversations with Vanessa. Dolores is getting a different kind of feedback now. Her daughter asks about her stepfather, and about her mother's day. She takes an interest in Dolores's music and tells her how much the kids are enjoying her newest CD.

"She does share, and she's always been like that; she's a wonderful girl."

What a difference an apology and a genuine expression of love can make. Dolores knows that her daughter had this dream of a cookie-baking grandma filling the kitchen with the aroma of freshly baked goodies and watching the little ones dance around the kitchen. Baking isn't her forte, but Dolores has come up with a great solution.

"I take instant cookie dough out and make cookies with the boys."

This seems to be working. Dolores tells me, "Vanessa says I'm really trying."

Dolores is fully aware of the debt she owes Alison.

"I've said to Alison, 'I just can't believe how thoughtful you are. You could say, "I am the good child; she is the bad one," and milk it for all you can, and you're not doing that.' "

Dolores grew up in a hard-luck situation, but her very good luck was to have daughters who could coach her on how to be their mother. Her firstborn posed the problem and her younger helped her solve it. She is grateful to them both.

"I do believe we are all on our own path and they got something from me, but they owe me nothing. They are on their own journey, and I am just grateful to be in their lives."

Listen to this sentence, spoken by a woman whose life has been a lonely journey. Carried in her mother's arms from her home as it was being overrun by a cruel enemy, raised with her kid sister in a family filled with sorrow and rage, and then orphaned in her twenties, Dolores had to invent herself twice. No wonder she had problems with conflict and intimacy. The miracle of Dolores's story lies in her daughters' determination to walk through life with her, and to teach her how to be their mother.

Actions Speak Louder Than Words

*"My father, I thought we weren't close, but now thinking about it,
I realize I'm much closer with him than I thought."*

Gary and his father never talked a lot, and he took for
granted all the time his father spent with him. He was
much closer to his mother. Then a surprising invitation
from his father forced Gary to pay full attention to his father's love, both when he was a boy and now, as a man. Fathers do not often emote. They are quiet around their
sons, and sometimes their feelings are not so easy to understand. But just as grown children's love is hidden in
plain sight, so often is a parent's.

Gary is a small, good-looking man. He is wearing
skintight shorts, a black top, stylish sneakers, and no
socks. It's a hot day, and we enjoy our iced drinks. Gary is
excited. He's been energized by an extraordinary event in
his family. He has always been close to his mother, who is
the strong personality in the family and the one with
whom he has spent many hours of his life, in person and
on the phone, discussing everything in the world. A partner in an international law firm, she traveled a lot and still
does. But she always made a point to spend time with him.
When traveling, she would do heroic feats in order to be
home for her son's special occasions. They still are close,
and they chatter endlessly with each other.

"We did trips together every year, and we still do,"
Gary says. But now that he is traveling with his boyfriend,
it's different. They went to a place where he had been with

his mom, and she sent an E-mail the day that he got back, saying, "Was traveling with him better than traveling with me?" Gary's mom was never judgmental about his sexuality, but she didn't seem interested in his finding a permanent partner. Gary thinks she was uncomfortable at the thought of him having a deep relationship with another man; that was where she drew the line, he believed. Maybe she was jealous of his getting close to another person— mothers of sons sometimes feel that way.

I have spoken with many gay young men and women, and they all find it easier to talk about their sexuality with their mothers—if they talk to any parent about it. When Gary came out to his father, he didn't get much of a response. Gary's father never expressed dismay to Gary, but his mother did report that his father was not happy. That didn't surprise Gary, since his father is profoundly conservative. Gary remembers him as a sad, repressed man who hated his work and drank. They spent time together, but they didn't talk much. His father lightened up a bit once he retired from a job he never enjoyed.

Today, Gary is elated about his father and thinks his father's actions show him to be more tolerant and accepting than he ever imagined.

"I'm dating someone now, and my father is the one who suggested we all go to dinner together. It's a very interesting time for me. I don't know if it's because he's retired and mellowed out a little bit."

His mother had called to say that his father had suggested dinner together, since they were all going to be in

L.A. for work in a couple of weeks. It was shocking to Gary, because he was reconciled to his father's tacit disapproval, and he was fascinated to hear his mother's tone of voice: She wasn't so enthusiastic.

Gary was excited at the prospect of this dinner, and a little intimidated. But it made him reconsider his dad's role in his life. Perhaps he had taken his father for granted and underestimated his love and affection. Gary now remembers that his dad was there for every sporting event, every band concert when he was young. "Every single one, he was there." His father turned up whenever Gary needed him—at games, to drive him to the dentist and the doctor—and he never missed a school parents' event. Although they didn't talk much, Gary could always count on his father.

His mother and he are more intimate; she confides in Gary about the pressures of her work and the disappointments in her marriage. Gary wants her to be happy, but he's not sure she ever will be. And like his mother, he had shrugged off his father's feelings. Now he is thinking twice about this man.

"I don't know if he did it out of a sense of obligation or because he genuinely wanted to, and it honestly doesn't matter. The fact that he made the offer is what matters to me," Gary says. "It's all very new and it's twisting everything, because if we'd spoken a week ago, I would have told you I'm closer with my mom and we have a great relationship. Now everything's changed."

~∾~

That is how easily children can reframe their memory of the past. In Gary's case, his father's simple gesture forced him to focus on the many ways in which his father had showed him his love over the years. Gary, like so many grown children, is more than ready to express the joy of mutual recognition. He always loved his father—that's part of the equation in most families—but now that love has gained new energy because of his father's act of acceptance.

Diane's mother's lessons of love and acceptance still instruct her daughter and husband, long after her death. Erin's father reformed himself and got his daughter back. Dolores's younger daughter showed her what she needed to do to save a precious relationship, and it worked. It is amazing how effective phone calls, cookie dough, or even a dinner invitation can be.

This chapter began with the very good news that grown children feel great love and gratitude toward their parents, even if we made a lot of mistakes when they were young, and even though they are trying to distance themselves from us now. I was surprised to learn how little it takes to improve the relationship with our grown children. We don't have to remake ourselves; we just have to listen to them and be mindful of what they are living through and adjust our behavior to that. We have to treat them like the adults they are. We have to give up the past, so that they can do the same.

Two things encourage this path. First, they love us, and they want our love. Second, not only do the small changes in our attitude make things easier; these changes can also help them understand and reframe the past. Our kids need to see us differently, not as the powerful puppet masters we used to be, but as ordinary people with ordinary weaknesses and flaws. If they gain some compassion and understanding, they may reconsider their view of the past. Sometimes they will appreciate things they had forgotten, and they may also begin to understand why we did the things they resented. We have the power to invite them home on a new footing. This is done through our words, our actions, our tone, and even our body language.

So long as we are alive, nothing is set in stone, neither our old habits nor our children's old resentments. Life is long, and the work of being a parent never ends.

3

One Size Doesn't Fit All

I have been ruminating about Tolstoy's comment at the opening of *Anna Karenina*: "Happy families are all alike; every unhappy family is unhappy in its own way." I think it was the novelist's way of telling the reader that stories about happy families are not interesting. I have not found that to be true. For me, happy families are fascinating because you can see the family members working and thinking about how to make things mesh. Perfect families do look alike, and that's because any family that makes you think it is perfect is covering up the truth. The effort sucks the energy and interest right out of the house, and it becomes boring. Sometimes I find myself wishing that I had a family like the ones I'm watching or hearing about: wonderful couples and perfect grown children, no conflicts, no problems. I know that their problems are none of my business, but I also have come to realize that I probably don't know the whole truth. Somebody is just working very hard to make a good impression.

Fights and reconciliations, pain and joy are the stuff of human existence. Expectations not met, feelings hurt, serious mistakes by everybody—what else is life? The interesting question is how to stay connected through the hard times and maintain the balance between closeness and distance that works for you and your grown children. Most important is to make sure that the bonds don't break.

Rubber bands litter my desk. They circle some door handles in my house. For years, I stored them on my wrist. When I was a girl, I used to play with them: pull out, snap back, pull out, snap back. Sometimes after too many pulls, they gave up and broke. This always came as surprise.

Families with grown children are like a collection of rubber bands. Imagine each relationship between two people in a family as being held together by one rubber band or another. No two relationships are alike. Parents find themselves in greater harmony with one child than with another. Temperament, gender, birth order, the time between children, events beyond our control—all these affect the bond we have with each child. Like those rubber bands, some relationships are stretched thin and some are very tight. That's the way families are.

⌁

The Cantor family is not without conflict; there are pulls and pushes, and bumps in the road will never go away entirely. Each of the Cantors' children presented them with different combinations of joy and worry. With three grown children and two strong-minded parents, there is complexity—and love—to spare.

Three Degrees of Closeness

What a shock it is to have a first son who is your opposite. His personality, his interests are so different from those of the rest of the family that it is hard to understand him and not so easy to appreciate him.

"Pete is Pete. Pete marches to the beat of a different glockenspiel," says Marty, Pete's father, a surgeon at a major medical center. Pete, the eldest of three, was always a challenge. He was an adventurer. It made his parents crazy, as they were always getting him out of scrapes. He loves risk. A firefighter and police officer, Pete is in the National Guard. He's been all over the world. Not to Iraq—yet—but his parents worry. The problems with Pete began when he was two and had the misfortune of getting first one sister and then another, just ten months apart.

Good little girls and an unruly older brother—a recipe for trouble. A cutup in high school, Pete tried college and lasted a couple of semesters.

"He went to Colorado and majored in the Grateful Dead," his mother says. So he moved back home for several months, and that was not fun for anyone. "He was working jobs like Jiffy Lube—you know, really crummy jobs—and was a pretty angry kid. Finally, we said, 'Pete, that's enough. You're much better off when you're someplace else.' " So he moved out and continued in lousy jobs for another year or so, until he joined the National Guard.

Marty was worried sick that Pete would come back in a body bag, afraid that he might lip off to some DI, who will kill him. Marty grins. "It turned out that Pete didn't have an authority problem: He just had a Dad problem." Pete graduated at the top of his class in basic training and went on to his military specialty, then graduated at the top of that class.

Pete is thirty-five now, and he finally graduated from college (it took him thirteen years). He married a woman ten years older than he, a concert musician, and they have two sons. They live on a big piece of land in Montana. Ruth, Pete's wife, is not tough enough with the boys, whom their grandparents describe as "Tasmanian devils." When Pete is away on active duty, Ruth has a hard time disciplining them. She is more of an absentminded professor; the kids can be tearing the house down, and she is tuned out. Pete is somebody you don't mess with, but when he's not home, all hell breaks loose. When Pete was deployed in

Europe a few summers ago, his parents invited Ruth and the boys up for six weeks. She didn't say, "I don't want to be with you for that long." She said, "Oh, thank you! Thank you!" and drove directly to their home. Did the grandparents discipline the kids? Oh yes, and they responded pretty well.

Even when Pete is home, his parents don't talk much with him. He is taciturn on the phone and distant in person. Marty and Louise tell me that of their three children, they feel least close to him. Although the Cantors tell their story in even tones, it's impossible to ignore the wide gap between who Pete is and who they are. Coming to the aid of Ruth and the boys plays a big part in their closeness, but Pete will always be Pete, his father and mother know.

Marty is a handsome man, compact and muscular. His light eyes command attention, and he has the demeanor of someone who is happy to be in charge. I can see why he has been such a successful surgeon—strong, direct, and sure of himself. He confesses to a temper, which is not hard to imagine, either. Louise is small and quiet, her short dark hair caps her head, and she has an air of quiet strength. Marty is pretty clear about his wife. "The one they don't mess with is Louise, because while Louise is quieter than I am, there is that 'You don't want to cross me, baby' about Louise."

⁓

The Cantors' two daughters are as different from each other as they are from their older brother. Melody is the conventional one. She married right out of high school and has two perfect sons, who are so well mannered that, at the ages of seven and eight, they sit quietly through the long Sunday-morning church services—quite a contrast to their Montana cousins. Louise feels very close to Melody. When she was pregnant with her first child, Melody was confined to bed for four months, and Louise spent every lunch hour with her, either on the phone or in person. Melody asked her to be there with her during labor, a highlight of Louise's life.

Marty and Melody are on a good footing now, although this wasn't always the case. "Melody and I sort of have a lippy relationship with each other," says Marty. "Occasionally, if I criticize her—which isn't very often, because she is a pretty good mom and employee and so on— I'll get lip back." Louise thinks Melody felt intimidated by Marty when she was a kid, but in the last couple of years she decided that as an adult, she can give him lip back. She no longer feels put down by her father's criticism. Marty thinks a lot of it has to do with her terrific sons. Melody thinks, If I gave birth to these kids and he thinks they are so perfect and wonderful, how can he be critical of me? Leave it to the grandchildren. Melody has been the good daughter, and her parents appreciate it. She's a far cry from her older brother or her younger sister.

Lori, the youngest, dropped out of school and got involved in the drug scene in her town. She lived at home and then left, and her taste in men was questionable. Her father describes the succession of boyfriends as "the kind you could find on Wanted posters in the post office."

Marty and Louise are thankful that Lori never married any of them. Throughout all the years of trouble, Lori stayed connected with the family. Her parents were simply not going to give up on her. Louise, in particular, has been very clear about this. "We're not going to cut the tie. You can act badly. We're not going to bail you out, but we're not going to disown you." It must have been extremely difficult to keep cool while watching Lori throw her life away.

"I can't imagine doing anything else. It's a blessing and a miracle that she'd finally had enough," says Louise.

After more than a decade, Lori moved back home, and she has turned her life around. The Cantors can't contain their pleasure. When she moved in, she broke her crack cocaine habit, cold turkey.

"I mean, her coming home was, for me, tinged with a certain bit of Oh my God, what are we getting into?" her mother says. It took a period of adjustment until Lori felt truly independent and nevertheless was mindful of her parents' needs and worries. She attended the local community college and is starting university next year. At first, Melody would not let the boys see her sister, because she didn't want them around a crack cocaine addict. When Lori finally demonstrated that she was drug-free, the boys got another loving aunt in their lives. Both parents are delighted.

"She cuts the lawn for us. We see her every day and talk with her every day. She's just an interesting gal, having done a complete one-hundred-and-eighty-degree change in the direction of her life," says Marty, who is proud of the sense of competence and confidence he now sees in Lori. She is discovering that if she works at something, good things will happen and she will feel better about herself. Better late than never, her grateful parents think.

Here it is in a nutshell: Pete, the aggressive bad boy; Melody, the perfect one; and Lori, the sinner—three such different personalities growing up in the same household. This family story makes you believe in nature over nurture. The parents had to learn to roll with the punches and to keep cool even when things were going rapidly downhill. But their three children have turned out pretty well. And so have their relationships with their folks.

"If you had a problem, whom would you go to?" I ask the parents.

Marty replies, "Depends upon the problem. If I want an executrix, it is going to be Melody. If I want to talk about a frustration at work, it's Lori. If I want to talk about how to fix my pistol, it's going to be Pete."

Marty and Pete get along best when they are together in Montana. Here's why.

"Well, Pete has got a lot of guns, and I grew up in a family in which, up until 1939, my father was a pacifist. They were very unhappy about my having cap guns as a kid." Marty smiles. "I've always been very interested in guns but never had any. But at his place, you can sit out on the front porch and shoot."

"And you love it," I say.

"I love it, and he loves that I love it."

Bingo. If there are words from a parent that characterize a solid relationship, it's that sentence: "I love it, and he loves that I love it." Here's a father and son whose values are diametrically opposed. But Marty loves sitting on the front porch with his son, shooting guns. Guns have been the bridge between the surgeon raised in a pacifist home and his activist, fighting son.

Things are more complicated for Louise, because she is not close to Pete, and she has had to deal differently with each of her daughters.

"I am torn between Melody and Lori. In different ways, I feel pretty equally close to both of them. I feel comfortable talking with both of them about problems. I can't pick one."

Marty and Louise have learned to accept the different degrees of closeness they have with their three grown children. It has taken a lot of work to sustain such different relationships, but they know it is paying off.

When Marty turned sixty, he and Louise woke up and saw thirty-five pink flamingos in the front yard, along with a goofy picture of Marty with a legend that said "He may be sixty, but he still acts silly." Louise didn't want any such attention when she turned sixty, so she and Marty left town for her birthday. When they got back, they walked into the living room and found sixty plaster sheep all around the room. Louise collects sheep.

Marty and Louise's grown kids are well into their thirties now. Their conflicts are getting resolved and things are settling down. Like many parents, they found the decade when their children were in their twenties the most taxing. It comes as a surprise that the decade when children get out of college, or at least leave the nest, is one of such conflict and disappointment. Many of us were in our twenties when we married and had children. We expected that our children would achieve the same mileposts at the same ages we did. Today, it takes longer for kids to grow up, and if we expect them to follow our timetable, we will be disappointed. Children are just not adults when they graduate from college, as Janice knows.

Gotta Go

It is hard on all parents when their grown kids don't have time for them. In their twenties, these young adults ask advice, but they don't take it; they call to check in and then get off the phone. They arrive home as adults and deposit their dirty laundry in the middle of the living room. Dirty clothes can sit there for days before the mother of the family gives in and does laundry. It is infuriating. They want our counsel, but they insist on making their own mistakes. They miss us, but they must be independent.

It brings to mind that moment when they were learning to walk. They would be ready to let go and take a step on their own, and then they would feel unsteady. Determined to accomplish this feat, they would launch themselves too fast and topple over. We cringed when they fell, but we had to let them do it without our help. Every fall made their footing more secure, and soon they stopped looking back at us for encouragement.

Janice and her husband have grown kids who are twenty-three and twenty-five. They find this decade excruciating. The kids want to be close, and then they disappear. They accept financial help without a thank-you, and they don't communicate much. Then unexpectedly, they are in touch, and it feels so good.

"Her first turkey took eight phone calls to me. It started at the market and then it was getting it thawed out and what do I do," says Janice. " 'Okay, he's had his bath and he's all dried off and he's been massaged with oil. Now I'm going to put him in the pan, but would he rather have his legs sticking up or down?' "

Janice and her husband live in the Midwest, and their two children have struck out on their own in New York, where they hope to make it as a rock musician (the son) and a set designer (the daughter). Since the kids come home only twice a year, the telephone is the family's central method of communication, and it is important to everybody. Many parents told me about how critical the phone connection is. Calls like the turkey call are good, very good. Janice, like many midwesterners, downplays her feelings, telling me, "It seems so minor, but it is wonderful, feeling needed."

The daughter isn't the only child to phone home for cooking tips. One Thanksgiving, their son called to ask his mom for his favorite sweet potato recipe. He was going to a dinner with a group and had to take a dish. He wanted to make Janice's sweet potatoes so he could eat them on the holiday. She gave him detailed directions and he followed the recipe and called to tell her all about it from the car. The sweet potatoes were a success, and then he had gone to a fund-raiser where they were serving bugs and insects, and he ate a scorpion on a toast point. "I knew I had to be there," he told her. "I tasted all kinds of things. I had rattlesnake and all sorts of things. It was terrific." Then came the awful phrase: "Gotta go!"

This is a sentence that parents dread. The kids are on the run, they're creating the own lives, they don't want to feel dependent, and they are not thinking about us. They do check in, but all too soon, it's "Gotta go." If Janice and her husband reach their son the day he comes home from a tour and he is in the right mood, he'll have a lot to tell and they will talk for quite some time. But if they don't catch him at that moment, it's "Oh yeah, it was fun."

Trying to have a genuine interaction on the phone with your grown children is a quintessential "eggshell experience." You don't want to push them, but a real conversation would be so sweet. One woman has such short talks with her grown son that her husband swears he could take a deep breath and hold it for the entire length of the conversation. Grown children know from the tone of voice when their mother or father wants to keep on talking, but they just can't accommodate them most of the time. Some understand that it makes their parents feel bad, but they get off the phone anyway.

Janice and her husband cannot afford to help their kids with their rent or give them an allowance. I don't think they would do that anyway, because they believe their children should make it on their own, especially if they want a life in the arts. They do pay for their health insurance and car insurance. This gives them peace of mind without making the kids feel dependent. They are not sure if their children value these contributions. They probably won't find out until the kids turn thirty, but they long for a response.

"We know at his age health insurance isn't important. Still, some real feedback would be mighty nice. We just need a few details, a few anecdotes, now and then," Janice says.

This is characteristic of kids in their twenties. It strains parents' patience. Getting through adolescence is hard enough, and then there is relief when they leave for college. At this new juncture, parents expect their children to act like adults. That is not happening these days. A new developmental stage, called "emerging adulthood," has been explored by social psychologists and the media. What they have found is that twenty-somethings are not really grown; they are not committing to a life's work, or to another person. They are floating through life, tasting and testing until they reach their thirties. It is frustrating for parents, who expect them to choose careers and mates, and who have been looking forward to an easy back-and-forth with their adult children.

Like so many parents, Janice and her husband are going to have to wait. Meanwhile, there are visits from the kids, when they sit at home and listen to music late in the evening and just talk. When their son was home last fall, he and Janice were on their way to get a bite to eat. Janice knows that her son loves the outdoors, and they were able to enjoy it together on this visit. "It was almost sunset and I drove out to this preserve west of town and took him up on this hill, and we just sat there and watched the sunset and talked. Nothing earth-shattering. No big news. As we were walking back down to the car, we turned around to look. The sun was below the horizon, but it was still light. We turned around and saw that the moon had just come up. He said, 'Mom, thank you.' " Such moments have to sustain Janice and her husband until their children reach their thirties. Meanwhile, they wait for the phone to ring.

Picture, Picture on the Wall

"Do you know how much you've hurt me? I love him.
I want to stand on a mountaintop and tell the world how much
I love him and that I found him. So when you tell me
to be quiet and shush, you make me feel like I don't belong."

This is a story about a picture that hangs in Douglas's mother's house. Like so many mothers, she has dedicated one wall in the dining room to framed photos of the family: her parents and her husband's, the uncles and aunts, the brothers, sisters, children, nieces, nephews, and grandkids. Douglas was so glad when he found his partner and was able to provide a picture of them to hang up on her wall. He had no idea how important that picture would become in the unfolding family drama.

At forty-seven, Douglas has dark, dark spiky hair, staccato speech, and the sculptured body of a middle-aged man who takes very good care of himself. He has expressive eyes, and there is drama in his every sentence. His tone softens when he speaks of love and his voice takes on an edge when he gets angry. Douglas has a razor-sharp delivery, but he's a big marshmallow inside. Douglas has had a hard life. His dad was given to rages.

"We would run out of the house in the middle of the night when he'd come home. We'd sneak out the back, get to a pay phone, and call our aunt and uncle to pick us up," Douglas says. He and his brother and sister made a great team. "We used to set traps for my dad. We would hear him come through the door and we would wire the stereo to the light switch. So when we hit the light switch, the stereo would blast, so he'd walk back out again."

It was not easy for Douglas, growing up in a tract-house neighborhood where religious conservatism was the order of the day. He was very close to his mother, who tried to shield him from harm. She comes from a Spanish-Portuguese family, and his father's family are Irish Catholics, so Douglas was certain that he was going to Hell. Suffering from panic attacks and agoraphobia, Douglas depended totally on his mother.

Over time and years of therapy, Douglas created a good life for himself. But it wasn't until he was in his middle forties that he found the love of his life, Bryan, a young man whose spirit meshes with Douglas's.

Douglas's family loves Bryan. The problem was that they didn't want to be reminded of him and his relationship with Douglas at family gatherings, or so it seems. It came to a head one Thanksgiving, when Douglas's mother took the photograph of Douglas and Bryan down from the dining room wall. He asked his mother where the picture was. She told him she had removed it at the request of his sister. Douglas was hurt, but he kept his mouth shut for a few days, and then he spoke honestly to his mother.

"I want you to know how much that bothered me, how much it hurt me that you took the picture down," he told his mother. She defended herself, saying that his sister didn't want her son to see the picture, because she might have to explain a gay relationship. Douglas felt that the family was suddenly aligning itself in a different direction. He was shaken because as long as he could remember, his mother had been his staunchest ally. Taking down that picture dealt a serious blow to their relationship, and over the next few weeks, Douglas found himself drifting away from her. He was miserable.

"I couldn't breathe. I wasn't comfortable in her home anymore." The photo of him and Bryan on her wall came to symbolize the acceptance and love that Douglas had counted on all his life.

Bringing home one's lover is a big step for anybody, but for gay men and women it looms as a critical stage of acceptance. Parents find it easier to deal with their grown children's sexuality in principle. But when there is a significant other, the reality of the relationship cannot be ignored. I have seen different gradations of acceptance, from ease and love to denial and anger. Douglas's family, despite all of this fuss about the picture, had been loving and accepting of him for decades. Sensing what a big deal it would be for them, Douglas had not brought home casual boyfriends. He was saving this big adjustment for that special someone. Now he discovered that although they loved Bryan, they couldn't manage full acceptance.

For Douglas, the situation was nonnegotiable. Taking the picture down destroyed his sense of being loved and accepted for the man he is. Douglas was not about to compromise on this. He wanted both his partner and his family. He knew that his mother was caught in the middle between him and his sister. When he talked to his sister, he found out that she did have a real problem with the picture, and it wasn't really about him and Bryan. It was about her son. She worried that he might be gay, and she didn't want to have any reminders of Douglas and Bryan on the walls of her mother's home. Douglas understood immediately, and then rose to his nephew's defense.

"If your son is gay, don't you dare do what was done to me. I was told, 'Put your feelings away. You're going to be a man. We're going to change you.' I won't let you do that to him." That was a loving promise, not a threat. But his sister was worried. She could not bear to see her son go through what Douglas had experienced.

"He won't, because he'll have you and me. He'll have positive role models," Douglas said.

Up went the picture, but it came down again at his father's birthday party. Douglas was adamant.

"Mom, you have to take a stand. It's important. This is your home. You make a decision. Either you're going to accept who I am, and who I'm with, or you're not. That's it. That's the bottom line."

Up it went again. Even though the battle of the picture was won, Douglas still had to take a stand with his father and his brother. They both wanted him to come to family events without Bryan. That was not about to happen.

"Either you guys start inviting him, or I'm not coming. His name and my name need to be on that invitation." Many conversations, many walks around the block, many deep breaths, and eventually they all came around. Bryan went to Douglas's father's birthday party and met the uncles; he went with Douglas to his nephew's christening. The net effect of all these battles is that Douglas got his mother back.

"I went over to her house Friday night just to hang out. I'm trying to spend more time there. She kept looking at me. 'Mom, what's wrong?' I said.

" 'Nothing. You're here.' I thought, Hmm, I think she finally gets it."

"And look what she got by really hearing you," I said when we talked.

"She's got me back in full."

Snap. Douglas recognized that it would take a major campaign for full acceptance in order to keep his family. He could have chosen to remove himself from the family, as his mother had removed the picture of him and Bryan. But he loves them too much, and he knows how much they love him. Douglas was explicit. Unless they accepted

Bryan, they would lose him. No stranger to conflict, he was certain of his mother's deep love for him. So he could risk the confrontation with the whole family, and his determination paid off.

Conflict in a family is scary. It takes a tremendous amount of confidence to lay your cards on the table the way Douglas did. Most people don't have the courage to fight, because they are afraid of permanently damaging family relationships. They use other means to deal with differences between them and their family members.

Angela has chosen an alternate route to family peace: She keeps secrets. Distance is her friend: Her parents are in Argentina, and she sees them infrequently. They learn only what she wants them to know about her life, and that suits her. Angela has made the grown child's compact: Don't ask; don't tell. This was common in my generation. Authoritarian parents were so nosy and pushy that grown children did not confide in them but presented a pleasant exterior instead. Physical distance can sometimes help families maintain harmony where conflicts exist beneath the surface.

All Alone by the Telephone

"Generosity, kindness, respect for others. They would always put us before they would put themselves. If my dad got some extra money,

he would buy presents for us instead of for himself. Those ways of
loving I have carried with me, and this idea that family is first,
and that love and family come before anything else—
after God, of course, but before work and money and everything else."

These are the lessons Angela cherishes from her parents. Angela came to America as a teenager with nothing but high school English, a scholarship to a good college, and a great ambition. Those first years were lonely and sad. She cried every night because she missed her family so much, but pain did not keep her from accomplishing her goals. She got a full scholarship to an Ivy League law school and then clerked for a federal judge. Her parents are very proud of her accomplishments and thrilled with her success. They do not know about her problems.

"The times I've been hurting the most—about a breakup or something of that sort—I haven't really talked to them about it. I got really depressed in law school. I waited to tell them for a long time, until it was too late. I told them when I had already decided to take a year off."

That shocked her parents, who asked, "Why didn't you tell us you were depressed?"

She couldn't, she told me. "You have to feel close and safe to confess sorrow and weakness."

Part of Angela's job has been to get them to accept and understand people who are completely different. Angela has introduced them to her wide variety of American friends, and she even took her best friend, a gay man, to visit them in Argentina. They are profoundly religious Catholics. Angela is still struggling with her religion. They don't discuss it, and her parents have no idea of how Angela spends her Sunday mornings. They don't have any idea of what she thinks about many things, and that is a relief to her.

She may feel close to her family, but she disagrees with them about religion, sex, and money. Physical distance is her ally. "Argentina is a very homogeneous country. I have become the person that I am because I left. If I had stayed, I would have been completely frustrated."

Angela relishes her privacy. "I grew up in a house where I shared a bedroom with my sister and doors were never locked. We were not allowed to close our bedroom doors, ever, unless like we were sick or something. So my parents were always in our business. They knew everything." Angela tells me that the maid was her mother's designated spy; she poked into their business, peeking into their purses and snooping on their conversations, and she told their mother everything. This would be enough to propel any strong-minded person to go to a new country. America is Angela's safety zone.

"I would have felt very trapped in Argentina, and I think that would have been reflected in every relationship, and I think we probably would have fought a lot. And who knows, if I'd stayed, I probably would have done what was expected and had a totally different life."

Angela's decision to dedicate her career to the legal problems of immigrants and the poor, instead of making a pile of money as a litigator, is a major source of family conflict these days. When her parents come to visit, they ask, "Well, why don't you just go into a downtown firm and buy a big house and buy a big car and be happy? Then pay off your loans. Why put yourself through the struggle? With your record, you surely could make partner." Angela has explained that free time, flexibility, and intellectual stimulation are more important to her than money. There is no question in Angela's mind about the career path she has chosen. But her parents do not mince words. One day, driving through a fancy neighborhood, her dad pointed to one of the mansions. "You could have that," he said. She replied, "Well, I don't want it; I don't need it." That ended one conversation but did not head off others. Those annual visits are hard.

"We are good for two weeks, then the third week they start driving me insane, and then the fourth week, I start getting sad that they're leaving." As much as she misses her parents, the geographical distance has enabled her to be herself and yet maintain a warm and affectionate relationship with them.

"Every interaction that we have is really positive, unless there's some tragedy or drama going on that I'm able to share with them." She doesn't share much, though, which both adds to her sense of being all alone and allows her to stay attached to her parents. This is the paradox of keeping your distance: You can keep secrets from your family, but then you can't lean on them. Angela believes this is a small price to pay.

"The reason why our relationship is good is because we only have the good."

Still, when she can't tell them what is going on, Angela feels lonely and isolated. "It's not like I don't want them to know. I just feel they wouldn't get it." Angela is glad that her parents did not follow her to America.

"Well, if they had come here with me, my growth would have been halted in some ways. I think it would have been a lot harder for me to detach from Argentina, from the culture, from the prejudices and judgments, so in that particular sense it would have been a little tough."

Angela's is a cautionary tale. It reminds us that our grown children are selective about what they tell us. We don't know what they don't want us to know. Nobody welcomes bad news from their children. We suffer with their sorrow, conflict, trouble, or pain. Sad communications remind us that we are only as happy as our unhappiest child. When a grown child tells us he hates his job, or that she is having trouble getting pregnant, or that her husband has asked for a divorce, we are plunged back into the time when we had responsibility for them. At least when they were young, we could wrap them in our arms. But now we don't have the power to help them. So, while the rest of the family may be coasting along, one sorrowful child brings back our helplessness in the face of that child's pain.

Parents think, I would gladly go through that instead of him. Parents blame themselves for a grown child's trouble. It comes with the territory. Still, when they do tell us their problems, we can take comfort in the fact that they have made the decision to include us in their lives, sharing the bad as well as the good.

The members of the families in this chapter are very different, and things in their lives are constantly changing. The complexity of all this is daunting, and some people wonder what's wrong with them. People think,

Why do I have trouble communicating, responding correctly?

Why aren't my children successful/married/considerate?

Why do I worry all the time?

You worry because you're parents. And remember that the people down the street have bad days, too. It is a big mistake to evaluate how we get along with our children by imagining the lives of people we know the least and admire the most. They have their problems, and their grown children can be breaking their hearts, as well. In this fragmented culture, families are our survival institution. Every family has its own miseries, and its own pleasures. The trick is to keep the bands from tearing, and if one does break, to pick up another band and get back into the game.

PART II

Big Children, Big Problems

4

WHOSE LIFE IS IT, ANYWAY?

"Put on a sweater. It's cold."
"But, Mom, I'm sixty years old."
"You're still my son."

Being an adult means that you don't have to listen to
your parents anymore. Grown children are exquisitely sensitive to this. Innocent comments from us can
make them resentful and defensive. What we expect to be
shrugged off with a "Yeah, Mom" is often taken as an assault. Who wants to be told what to do? We don't, and neither do our grown children.

The impulse to give even the smallest tidbit of advice is almost impossible to resist, especially when we want to help our grown kids, who wouldn't be the people they are today were it not for the advice we raised them with. Right? Wrong. Not giving advice is one of the most difficult tasks of parenting adults. We give friends advice, and we advise our spouses, so why not our grown children?

Think of the playground seesaw. When we first played on it with our kids, we were so much bigger that we could control their ups and downs with our longer legs. We were in control and we able to give them a fun and safe ride. Now their legs are probably longer than ours, but in their minds, we are still the tall ones. When we tell them what they should do, they feel small and powerless all over again. That is why even the smallest, unimportant tidbit of advice raises hackles. Women in their sixties, who are grandmothers themselves, regaled me with stories about their ninety-year-old mothers, who still call to offer advice or ask questions.

"I think the weather's not good enough for you to drive today. I can't believe you're going to drive."

"Do you have your telephone?"

"Have you had your hair cut?"

"Here I am at sixty-five," said Peggy, "with a ninety-five-year-old mother telling me what to do. I am not yet independent." She is not amused by this, however she may laugh, and, like many women of my generation, she has done her best to let her children decide not only when to get their hair cut and whether to drive under icy conditions but also whom to marry, which house to buy, what to feed the grandchildren, and how to live their lives. The short version of my advice about advice is:

Don't give it;

They don't like it,

They don't want it,

They resent it.

My teachers taught that God selected the Ten Commandments (from among hundreds) because they are the ten most often broken. The eleventh commandment—Thou shalt not give your grown children advice—is like the first ten: extremely hard to keep. Of course we want to give our children the benefit of our experience. Why shouldn't we? And sometimes we desperately want to head off whatever disaster we can see them heading toward. But the more important the advice, and the closer it hits to home, the more it divides our children from us.

What happened in the years between the time they listened to our advice and now? They grew up. Today, their autonomy and our control are in direct conflict. This dynamic is not new in human history. In fact, rejecting advice from someone in authority goes back all the way to Adam and Eve. It could have been curiosity that made Eve take the apple, or it could have been the insidious influence of the snake. But perhaps Eve was thinking, What does He know? I'm sick of listening to Him. Adam and I are grown-ups and we'll do what we please. And so the

history of human adults begins with Adam and Eve breaking the bonds of God's control. Think of it from God's
point of view. If God hadn't given the first humans this
advice, they would still be in the Garden of Eden. God just
wanted to protect them from the Tree of Knowledge. This
eccentric reading of Genesis does underscore the point
that even good advice makes trouble in the family.

⌇

Norma, at seventy-six, knows that she is not in charge of
her kids, but she has trouble holding her tongue, and it
has created havoc with her firstborn son. Her excellent
advice has nearly destroyed their relationship.

The High Cost of Good Advice

Norma is lively woman who radiates energy. Her skin is
weathered and her gray hair is cropped close. A small
woman, she wears colors as vivid as her language. Her enthusiasm and idealism bubble. She is a good talker, and
she's opinionated. Norma has the kind of delivery that
makes her sound as if she always gets the last word, even
though she does not believe that of herself. An idealist and
an English professor, Norma taught literature at a conservative Christian college, but her contract was not re-
newed because the dean didn't approve of her going on
television and praising the Episcopal Church for appoint-
ing a gay bishop. That sums Norma up.

Norma has four children, who range in age from fifty-two to forty-six. She divorced her husband when the kids were teenagers, and she supported them until they grew up and struck out on their own. It was a hard life, and Roger, her eldest, was always testy and difficult. These two strong personalities clashed many times when Roger was young, but they still were close. When her husband remarried, Norma encouraged Roger to get to know his father's new wife. But Roger never got along with his father, and he would not visit with them. The new wife called Norma and asked her help, because she could not convince Roger to come over for dinner. Norma agreed to put in a word with Roger, believing that every child needs both a mother and a father. When Norma suggested that he accept the invitation, Roger shook his head. Norma persisted, saying, "I don't ask you to do many things."

Roger was cranky about it, but finally he agreed. He went over that evening at 5:00 P.M., and he still had not come home by midnight. Norma waited up for him. He returned in a great mood.

"One thing I've got to say about the old man is that he really knows how to choose women," Roger said. Norma was delighted, because she really wanted Roger and his father to have a relationship. One dinner is a small thing, and that was about the maximum amount of advice Roger could take from his mother.

The crisis between mother and son happened at his sister's wedding. Living in Idaho and working as a stone-mason, Roger is not given to conversation, and he has a short fuse. Norma was aware of his drinking problem, but there wasn't much she could do about it. As they were leaving her daughter's house for the wedding and the reception, Norma suggested that they take her car instead of his truck. She handed him the keys and they drove off together. But he drank a lot at the reception. So when they got to the car to drive home, Norma said,

"Roger, give me my keys, because you have had too much to drink."

"No, I'm okay," he said.

Norma was adamant.

"No, I am not going to drive with somebody who has had too much to drink." Although it was a short ride to the house, the road was winding, and she could imagine Roger hitting a tree. She grabbed the keys from him and said,

"You drink too much and you need to do something about it."

Roger was furious. He got up early the next morning and left for Idaho without a word.

Norma looks at me and shakes her head. She is sad and puzzled.

"That was it. I tried to call him to apologize and he hung up on me," she says.

Five years later, Roger has not forgiven his mother. Norma learned that Roger has been in AA for three years, and he is completely dry. He apologized to her, as AA prescribes, but she still can't get through to him.

"I love him dearly, but it's my fault," she tells me.

His brother and he exchange E-mails almost daily, and Roger's two sisters want to get mother and son together. This past Christmas, Norma visited her daughter, and Roger came down from Idaho. He stayed with his brother. The last evening he came over to his sister's house and he and Norma sat up talking late into the night.

"He is very formal with me. He used to kid me, you know. It's just not the same." Norma hit a nerve years ago, and she is still paying for it.

Norma is devastated about Roger and has come to recognize the paradox of good advice: The more correct it is and the closer to home it cuts, the more you are resented for giving it. Norma admits that she's opinionated, and she has tried to work on it. She has apologized to Roger many times and has tried to reach out to him.

"Well, one day I called him and said, 'We just need to talk a little bit.' He got off the phone as fast as he could." If Norma had been wrong about Roger's drinking, he might not have joined AA and stayed sober. The problem is that Roger will not be controlled and judged. That's what he hears in his mother's voice. "I want to make my own decisions and I want to be in charge of my own life," he told her.

She feels guilty about that incident with the car keys, and also about having kept silent for so many years about the drinking. In this family, guilt is a scalpel, separating flesh from flesh. Norma feels guilty about Roger's drinking problem. Such regrets hound us when our grown children have problems. Roger must feel terrible about being a disappointment to his accomplished parents, and about not being nice enough to his mother. When one person feels guilt and the other feels badly treated, both retreat. The gap gets hard to breach. The shared burdens of guilt and resentment weigh heavily on this mother and son, making communication and closeness difficult.

Roger could forgive Norma for pushing him to have dinner with his dad, but for his mother to cut to the heart of his drinking problem, anxious and afraid for their safety, was not acceptable. Norma grieves this loss. She can't figure out what to do. Roger is her first child, and sure, she is difficult, but so is he, and she loves him dearly. Here's the lesson she takes from this.

"Each kid is different. But each child is a gift, and I have to be careful to preserve the gift, because look at what happened with Roger, and he'd been so good to me. I've seen it happen overnight with other parents, too. You have to remember you're treading on dangerous territory when it's intergenerational."

Norma's epitaph for this relationship is sad. "I have cried over this, but I have to be myself, but it's gotten me in trouble. And in my old age, am I going to be less myself? The answer is no."

I don't think Roger's problem with his mother is necessarily about her personality. She was the same opinionated woman when he was young, and they were very close then. His anger, I think, is about the fact that she delivered a difficult truth, and he is blaming the messenger.

※

Efforts to exert control push grown children away. This is a hard lesson. We can no longer control them, but we have to keep perfect control of ourselves. That does not seem fair. It isn't fair. But time is on their side, not ours; they will outlive us. They can and will withdraw from us if things are tense. This reality may help us to stay cool. Wise people have offered some strategies for turning down the volume of these interactions before parents run into trouble.

If a phone call is getting tense, make believe you hear the doorbell ringing and get off the phone. That will keep the conversation from deteriorating.

If an E-mail from a grown child or an in-law makes you angry, it's okay to write a reply, but save it for a day and reread it before sending it. You would be amazed at what twenty-four hours can do for cooling down your tone.

Want to write a letter? Do it, and then file it in your drawer under *F,* for *furious.* Think twice about writing letters that express judgments and advice you would not offer in person. I know a man who has kept a letter his mother wrote him forty years ago, in which she warned him that he was drinking too much. He never listened to her, but it still makes him fume every time he thinks of it.

If you haven't been able to hold things together and communications have become difficult, there's another tactic: Keep at it. Leave loving and short messages on his voice mail, just reminding him that you love him; send kind notes via E-mail, just keeping her up to date, with no demand for a reply. Send a postcard, a note, something that says "I love you and I don't want to lose you." That helps to keep the door of reconciliation open.

My Way or the Highway

*"We're not close. She doesn't know what I'm doing every day,
and she certainly doesn't know my feelings about things."*

The less control you have, the louder you shout, and the
louder you shout, the less control you have. We cannot
control our grown children, no matter what we wish, no
matter how passionately we care. Because Celine's mother
is so intemperate in her expressions and actions, she high-
lights the difference between advice and control. Many
grown children are allergic to even simple advice, but Celine's mother is the archetype of the controlling parent.

The first people in the family Celine's mother fired
were her in-laws, strong-minded immigrants who kept to
the old ways and were unkind to her. Here's a typical story.
Celine's paternal grandmother is a great cook. She would
sniff as she came into Celine's mom's kitchen—not to admire the wonderful smells, but to criticize her poor cooking. Her husband's siblings all distanced themselves, and
some families moved to cities far away. When Celine was a
little girl, her mother gave her husband an ultimatum:
"Break off with your parents, or I'm leaving—and I'm
leaving the baby with you." Given that choice, Celine's father stopped seeing his parents, who virtually disappeared
from Celine's life. She didn't miss them—they weren't especially nice to her, either. Celine's problem isn't over the
loss of these grandparents. It's her mother, who often
gives an unfortunate choice: My way or the highway.

Her explosions drive Celine crazy; they may look like

advice from her mother's point of view, but to Celine, they are all about control. Celine recalls what she refers to as "the four incidents." The first two happened when she was a kid, and Celine shrugs these off now, because she thinks her mother had a right to be upset about her behavior in junior high and high school. But when she grew up, these eruptions were another matter.

Celine was always drawn to literature, and she was admitted to the state's top university, one with an excellent English department. Her mother had other plans for her. She had researched the employment situation in their area and decided that Celine would be better off getting a degree in computer science. When Celine told her parents she wanted to study English, a battle royal ensued, and they forced her to go to tech school. Parents have been forcing their children to follow their advice about careers since the beginning of time, but it burns as much today as it did in the past. Celine did eventually go to graduate school in literature, and she loves what she is doing. The biggest explosion happened when her mother learned that Celine's fiancé already had a child and that Celine was going to become a stepmother.

"When she found out about the daughter, she told my dad she was going to change the will and disown me. I was living at home at the time. She made me go through and label everything in the house that was mine, so she could send it to my fiancé's home and never see me again. I never would have believed it, until she was basically calling the attorney to get me out of the will."

Celine's mom's concern about her becoming a stepmother was not unwise, but her behavior was an effort to control Celine. Advice is different from control.

Advice sounds like this: "Maybe you should consider how you are going to feel about being a stepmother." (In fact, Celine doesn't care for that role.)

Control sounds like this: "I disown you."

Fortunately, that's not the end of the story.

"Maybe a week after disowning me, she came to me and apologized. She said she wanted to have a relationship with me, so she was going to work this out in her own mind." Her mother explained that she went ballistic when she heard about the stepdaughter because it made her think Celine might not have any children of her own. She had always wanted grandchildren, and this might mean that she wasn't going to have any.

Celine's mother realized she had gone too far. Of course she did not want to lose her daughter. She was just out of control. Fortunately, she was able explain what had been going on in her mind. This did not remedy a life-long pattern of explosive incidents, but it kept Celine in her life.

Grown children have a hard time telling the difference between an innocent remark and parental control. If we offer to help them buy a car or a house and make comments about their decisions, they get furious. We get hurt—after all, we were just trying to be helpful, and we didn't mean to criticize. The problem is that such words bring back the rage a daughter felt when she wasn't allowed to wear her favorite Goth outfit to a family bat mitzvah or the fury a son felt when he was kept home from a football game to finish a term paper. This kind of discipline and control was part and parcel of our unending effort to form them into acceptable members of society. In general, they are grateful to us for helping them grow into the people they are today, but the slightest reminder of the old days, when we exerted power over them, incites them to rebel, refuse, and finally repudiate.

Doris and her son are close but distant at the same time. Their annual trips keep them together. A set of rules set by Doris's grown son are in place on these vacations. If they were also followed at home, perhaps things would be easier for them both.

The Fixer-Upper

"We joke about how I can never quit giving advice, because I just love this little being so much."

This little being is thirty-eight years old. Doris wanted to tell me about the wonderful camping weekends she and her son take each year. Here's what they do. They drive to Yosemite National Park. They build campfires. On the first night, they dive into the freezing lake; the next day they climb a mountain, and her son cooks the traditional camping-out dishes from his childhood. The best part for Doris is the talks. Oh, for those rare moments when you actually kick back and just chat away with your son. Here is what makes these trips possible: "It's a spoken agreement where you won't venture too far into getting heavy about something, and if you do, the other person has permission to say, 'Back off a little, there.' " At the end of the weekend, they reserve the same cabin for the next year. As long as they abide by the rules, this tradition will continue.

For the rest of they year, they are not close, even though he lives a mile or so up the road from his mother. They rarely speak. And they have taken occasional months-long "vacations" from each other. Doris cannot keep her mouth shut. She feels compelled to improve him.

Her life story helps to explain this. Doris was a senior in high school when she got pregnant, which was a disaster, because she was planning to go to a university and become a poet. She could not get an abortion (this was thirty-nine years ago), and so she and her boyfriend rented a house on a beach miles from home and lived there while they awaited the baby, who was born on Christmas Eve. Doris had put him up for adoption, but the adoption agency permitted the parents a ten-day waiting period before the decision was final. The night they got home from the hospital, the boyfriend offered to take care of the baby and support them so that she could fulfill her dream and attend university. She accepted his offer, and they married two days later. The best man was carried in his mother's arms. The hospital staff was delirious.

Doris's story reflects the decade of the sixties: She got pregnant, couldn't get an abortion; they put the baby up for adoption, then decided to keep him. They became hippie schoolteachers and raised their son according to their countercultural beliefs.

"I had such ideals and this little being was like a sponge. He was like an experiment. He was so responsive that you could tell when you were doing it right and doing it wrong."

This was a wonderful period for Doris, in part because it confirmed her view of herself.

"I'm a very helping person; I'm a rescuer. I like to fix things. And I'm a cheerleader. He was always so willing to do things. I had a companion, someone telling me that I was valuable. It was a very meaningful time, because my life suddenly became worth living."

Being the subject of one's parents' educational experimentation is not necessarily easy on a child. The boy had a hard time finding himself in high school and college. He never graduated from either (he got his GED) and now he makes a good living as a contractor. Doris understands the reason why he is so distant from her.

"The whole time I was raising him, it was obvious to me that I was making a big difference in his life. Now I still get the urge to give him advice, but it's no longer appropriate. We have had many conversations about that, he and I, about how we are going to separate from each other. How do we back off?"

I think the real question for Doris is this: "How do *I* back off?" Doris can't stop herself. She calls him up and tells him that he has gained too much weight and should go on a diet; she urges him to join her gym; she makes comments about his girlfriends and the fact that he never finished school. She is still trying to be the teacher/mother.

"It is hard to let go. It's hard to not want to keep giving advice, because I still think I could help him."

Every time Doris tries this, her son edges away from her. She gets teary as she tells me how much she loves her son and how she pines to be the mommy she once was. It is a tribute to his affection for his mother that her son agrees to the yearly trip. If only they could import the Yosemite Accords into the other fifty-one weeks a year, Doris might not find herself weeping over a past she cannot reclaim.

Shredded-Tongue Syndrome

*"If you tell somebody what to do and it doesn't work,
it's always your fault. But if you just make them think about
the problem a little longer, they think you're a genius."*

Shredded-tongue syndrome appears when advice comes to mind but is not shared. Bloody-cheek syndrome occurs when criticism is about to jump out of a parent's mouth but is stopped. Since there is no way to offer criticism that doesn't make grown kids furious, here are some of the tips I heard from tactful parents.

One father gives advice by asking a question: "What will make you happy?" That is all he says, and it works. If this goes against your personality, consider calling family members or friends when you need to vent. A woman I know has this relationship with her fellow mother-in-law. They criticize their children to each other and complain about how the kids are ruining the grandchild. When they feel better, they laugh and remind each other that this conversation never took place.

If you feel you must say something, couch it in terms like these:

"Some people might think . . ."

"Here are some ways to consider the problem. . . ."

"This might sound silly, but . . ."

"Have you considered . . ."

"I had a friend who . . ."

Whatever words we choose, the task at hand is to make our children understand that we aren't there to interfere. They are exquisitely sensitive to spoken language and to body language. Our words, the look on our face, a glance exchanged between parents, a voice that tightens on the phone—these do not go unnoticed. Bringing home the important person in their lives causes them tremendous anxiety (as it did for us); talking with us about the choice of a house or a job puts them on the defensive. When our anxiety is high, we may scare them off. Many parents are hurt that their grown children don't take them seriously enough. Others are angry. "I brought her up—she should listen to me!" they may say. These feelings are legitimate, but they are not helpful. That is why we have spouses, friends, and relatives of our generation, people to whom we can let off steam when things get tense.

Tragedy's Lesson

Tragedy was Ginger's teacher. She cannot afford to lose either of her daughters. She already lost a child. Her son died in a car accident when he was nine. Adding to that sorrow is the fact that her younger daughter, who was sixteen at the time, was driving the car. Ginger was distraught, but just a few days after the funeral, she turned to her daughter and said, "I don't hold you responsible, because it was an accident. It could have been anybody."

"I just saw her face lighten," Ginger tells me. How did Ginger summon the love and courage to forgive her and to tell her that so soon after the accident?

"I saw that I could lose another child, psychologically. I remember one time in the middle of the night, a couple of weeks after the accident, I went to her room and I got in bed with her. It makes me cry to think about it. She comforted me, you know, and she saw me as a person, not a parent."

Ginger's advice is impeccable.

"The parent must recognize that their grown children are adults, and not treat them as children." Ginger says

that even when they come to you for advice, it is important to stay cool. And if your children ask you,

"Mom, what did you do when . . ." or

"How did you feel when . . ." or

"What was your solution to . . ."

they are not asking directly for advice. Family stories
are not threatening; they are like Aesop's fables—but the
listener gets to make up the moral at the end. And when
children come out and ask a question, it's always a good
idea to preface your answer by saying,

"You know, it might be worth taking a look at . . ." or

"I once had a friend who . . ." or

"I heard about somebody who . . ."

Ginger reminds me that Ann Landers used to say *should*
is a terrible word.

Ginger has put this into practice for years. Her daughter, at twenty-five, was thinking about marrying a man
who was twenty years older. Ginger was horrified at the age
gap, knowing there would be serious problems when her
daughter was sixty. She didn't preach, but she did lay the
issues out in a calm manner. Because she thinks the world
of this man, and communicated that to her daughter, the
advice to think twice about the age gap did not create hard
feelings. Her daughter decided to marry him anyway.

Ginger admits that she was tempted to say, "This is
a terrible idea. You mustn't marry him." But she knew it
was not her choice. These days, Ginger revels in her
daughter's happiness with her older husband and young
child, even though some of her worries are proving well

founded. Her son-in-law gets exhausted running after the baby, and he really wants to retire, which he cannot afford to do, with a wife and baby. Ginger could not have changed the outcome of the romance, and she realizes that giving advice and criticism would have damaged her relationship with her daughter. She knows that grown children are suspicious of our need to control them. If they experienced that control when they were young, they are supersensitive now. "So the parent has to do something that really clearly shows that they're not trying to judge," she says.

Long before books and articles identified the period in a young adult's life between graduating from college and becoming established, some time in one's thirties, Ginger understood what was going on. It turns out that this decade is good training for us; it accustoms us to a bit of distance from our children. Once they are established (usually after the thirtieth birthday), married or not, in a good job or not, they are getting ready to develop an adult—adult relationship with us. "If you use the decade between college and real adulthood to convince your children that you're not there to interfere and impose your ideas on them, good things can happen," says Ginger.

"I found a new, wonderful connection with my daughters since they got married, and particularly since they had children. You know, we are all parents, grand- or otherwise. As any mother of a young child would say, there's nobody else who is as interested in how he slept last night as the grandmother. That is a great opportunity for parents and children to cement their bonds—over those grand-children."

Tragedy taught Ginger this lesson: Nobody can afford to lose a child, literally or psychologically. That's part of what makes it so hard to sit still when problems arise and we know the solution. Remember when we went to the movies when we were kids? Sometimes we couldn't resist calling out to the characters on-screen, *"Watch out. The witch is around the corner!"* When we feel like doing that with our grown children, it helps to remember that we got through crises without taking our parents' advice. More important, if we keep our mouths shut now, they will make their own decisions and learn from their mistakes, just the way we did.

5

IN-LAWS, STEPPARENTS, AND OTHER ALIENS

The number of people each of us descends from is enormous—four, eight, sixteen, etc., ancestors. Each of us has a vast genetic heritage, which explains the wide variations among members of today's nuclear family. In the past, families lived and multiplied and died in close proximity. A strange characteristic in one child could be attributed to a weird uncle or cousin who lived in the same town. More important, there was usually an aunt or uncle who understood us a little better than our parents did. When we were making them crazy, they could send us off for a visit. We learned that in every family there are wide variations in temperament and talent. So you could always find a relative who was pathologically shy, just like your brother, or who really preferred working with her hands instead of reading, just like your sister. It took some of the heat off the necessity for each child to conform to expectations of outstanding performance and behavior. We lost this in the era of the nuclear family.

Today, we have again begun dealing with extended families that are enlarged, this time through divorce and remarriage. New relatives add another kind of complexity. Patriarchs who have been accustomed to gathering the clan at their table on holidays find themselves negotiating fine lines of loyalty with grown children and their in-laws, as well as older grandkids.

Negotiations over who goes where on Thanksgiving, Christmas, Easter, and Passover can rival international treaty talks. A sister-in-law who is used to having her brother and his wife at Thanksgiving is hurt when they stay home because all the grown kids and their spouses can come to them for a change. A grandmother of eighty-five who remarries may suddenly draw close to her new husband's family, leaving her own grown children and grandkids feeling abandoned.

Adding strangers to the family always changes things, and keeping the enlarged family on an even keel and all the relatives in a friendly frame of mind takes work. It is not easy, and the lessons we learned from the old nuclear-family model do not always translate well for today's sprawling families.

＊〜＊

Two elements make all the difference between ease and misery with in-laws and stepfamilies: chemistry and character. If the chemistry with the new relative is good, then character may not be called upon. If you are naturally drawn to someone, it is not hard to enjoy that person's company, to feel warmth and to be naturally pleased to see him or her. When the chemistry is off, character may help to carry the day. Character shows up when we put our feelings on the back burner and make an effort to forge a strong relationship, anyway.

Of course, it is best if you have both. Good chemistry is easy to recognize. One woman told me that when she met her son's girlfriend, she had the strange feeling that she was talking to herself. They think alike and they have travel experiences and values in common. She loved this young woman on sight. She feels wonderful that her only child, a son, has chosen someone who is so easy for her to love. Good for her and for the family. That is chemistry.

Then there are people who are not so sure about the prospective daughter- or son-in-law. Another woman liked her daughter's boyfriend just fine, but she worried that he didn't have the energy and ambition of the rest of the family. Years later, the son-in-law exceeded everybody's expectations, and the mother was glad that she had not expressed her concerns to her daughter. That is good character.

Peggy, the woman in the next story, was lucky. She and her mother-in-law had both.

Won't You Be My Neighbor?

"This is where my daughter-in-law lives, and we're still speaking."

Peggy has three grown children and three grandchildren. For many years, she lived next door to her mother-in-law in their leafy university town. When they moved home after graduate school, Peggy and her husband were given his parents' house, in which his grandparents had married, raised their children, and died. Her husband joined his father's business, and his folks moved into a small house across the driveway from the big one. Astonishingly, it worked out well for everyone.

"My husband's mother would walk down the driveway with her friends as she went past our house and into hers," Peggy says. Her windows were often open, and one day she heard her mother-in-law say to a friend, "And this is where my daughter-in-law lives, and we're still speaking," Peggy grins as she continues. "She was fabulous, a real character. She knew where to draw the line, and my kids had that example of extended family: close but not too close." Peggy adored her mother-in-law, and so did the children. "The kids went to grandmother's house when I wasn't home. She was a charming woman. They had a wonderful relationship with her."

"How did she treat you when the kids were small? Was she accepting of your ways or did she tell you how to raise them?" I ask.

"No, she never told me how to raise them."

"She knew intuitively?"

I could hear the warmth in Peggy's voice when she replied, "Oh, she was wonderful. Everything I did was great."

But was it perfect? Is anything perfect?

"The only argument we ever had with her was over a cleaning lady. I had found this wonderful cleaning lady who also baby-sat, fed the dog, did all these great things. She was envious! She propositioned the cleaning lady to clean her house as well as mine."

Peggy describes one other fly in the ointment: competition over her husband's time and attention. After she was widowed, Peggy's mother-in-law would keep an eye out for her son just around the time he was expected home. Peggy was counting the minutes until her husband arrived, so he could help her with the kids. But his mom would pop out of the house and stand in the driveway to catch her son's attention before he went home. This got on Peggy's nerves, but she admits it is a small gripe in the context of her mother-in-law's love and acceptance.

Peggy's own mother, on the other hand, is a flinty, strong-minded ninety-five-year-old woman, who just about ruined a recent family Christmas dinner because her grown granddaughter had not set the table with the bone china she prefers. She calls Peggy and goads her, and although Peggy and her husband take good care of her and love her, Peggy finds her mother a bit of a challenge. She is who she is, and she will always be.

Peggy was lucky to have such a good model in her mother-in-law. This fine woman clearly loved Peggy, so good chemistry was there at the start. Her generally accepting and appreciative manner set the standard for Peggy's relationships with her own grown children. Her mother-in-law had only sons, so she knew that her relationship with Peggy was crucial in staying close to the next generation.

⁀✀⁀

Mothers of men have a special burden and opportunity when their sons marry. Marion worked out things beautifully with her first daughter-in-law: They love each other. Then she faced a terrible reality, not uncommon today, when her son divorced the daughter-in-law she loved. Marion made excellent use of her good manners to weather this storm. She remains close to the daughter-in-law she loves. Her good character helps her deal with her difficult daughter-in-law, who is married to her younger son.

Mrs. Manners

"I have worked on this relationship the whole time, and it's working. It's hard work, but it's working."

Marion, a handsome white-haired woman of seventy-two, met her husband when they were graduate students, more than fifty years ago. They fell in love immediately and were engaged before he took her home to meet his formidable mother. The two women bonded and were close all his mother's life. When Marion moved with her husband to his small town, she had one rule: Her new husband could spend as much time as he wanted with his parents, but she would always accompany him. They kept to this rule, she explains, "because we felt they should accept us as a couple." Marion recognized that her husband had been very close to his parents, and she wanted to gain full membership in his family.

When Marion's eldest son married, Marion was determined to make the relationship with his wife work, because, like many mothers of sons, she knew that closeness with her son's family depended on her daughter-in-law. Things couldn't have turned out better. She and Donna hit it off immediately, and they were very much a part of each other's lives for twenty years. "It was a wonderful relationship and still is," she says.

Marion's holiday gifts were always just right, and there never was any serious conflict. Marion and her husband had easy access to the two grandchildren. Even though they lived in different cities, they were very close.

Marion was heartbroken when this marriage fell apart. Her son and Donna had been married twenty years. There was never a problem about access to the grandchildren, who were nearly grown. Because of Marion's innate sense of what is right, and her wish to experience no bumps with them, she continued to nurture the bonds with Donna. Marion loved Donna, and she was sorry that things would never again be the same. The relaxed back-and-forth between generations that had delighted her vanished.

Marion relies on her good manners to stay in appropriate and loving contact with her former daughter-in-law. When Donna's mother died of cancer last fall, Marion immediately picked up the phone and called. It felt perfectly natural. "I am not her mother, but I am probably her closest friend of my generation." They had a good, short conversation, and at some level the relationship still holds, "But my son comes first," Marion says.

This is a tricky maneuver. As much as she loves Donna, Marion is totally loyal to her son, so she cannot allow herself the kind of intimate relationship they used to enjoy. For example, the first time they saw each other after the separation was at a tennis match where the eldest grandson was playing. Instead of sitting next to Donna, as she would have in the old days, she placed herself between her son and her husband. She did, however, get up and hug Donna. "We both knew what the other was feeling without ever saying a word."

That was a sad little dance for Marion, but her upbringing tells her where to sit, and when to stand. Marion communicates to Donna in many ways; she drops her occasional notes, greets her warmly at family events, and she never talks to her grandchildren without saying, "Give my love to your mom." Marion can see the future, and it is one of increasing separation from her dear Donna.

"She recently sold the house and moved into a condo. I don't know if I'll ever see her new home," says Marion, who is sad that she has lost her good daughter-in-law. She continues to deal with the problematic one, who will probably stay married to her younger son forever. That daughter-in-law seems to wax hot and cold about her husband's parents, and she is not happy to share her children with them. Marion does better than she might have with this daughter-in-law, because her success with Donna has helped her understand that problems with difficult in-laws are not all her fault.

You don't have to be an old-fashioned woman to have Marion's determination. But there is a big difference between loving a daughter-in-law and missing her and disliking a daughter-in-law and gritting your teeth to hold on to the relationship with a grandchild.

Triumph of the Will

"If it weren't for the baby, this would be over."

Connie took an instantaneous dislike to the girl her son had chosen. Time has proven her first impression right. The couple soon divorced, but being right is no help at all. Connie grits her teeth and keeps the peace with her former daughter-in-law. If she doesn't toe the line, she knows she will lose her granddaughter.

Connie has a vivid way of expressing herself, and she is full of energy. Married four times, she has four children, two by her first husband, and two by her third.

"I call the husbands 'the good, the bad, the ugly, and the last.' " Last is really last, she tells me. She doesn't plan to marry again. Connie has kept up good relations with her first husband, the father of the two older children. Connie and her first husband need each other's support in order to deal with the situation they face with their son, Mark, and his ex-wife. Among her four kids, Connie's relationship with Mark was always the most difficult. The eldest child, he took off when he went to college and essentially left home.

"He was so pissed off about the breakup of my marriage with the third husband," Connie explains. In the aftermath of that divorce, Connie moved the family from a twenty-two-room Victorian house in New England to student housing in a university town. Mark did not have a clue as to what the younger children and Connie were experiencing with this man (a decade later, his younger siblings finally began opening up about their abusive father), and he was furious with his mother. Connie was intimidated by Mark's anger.

"I tended to follow his lead, which meant there were great long periods of noncommunication between us." He came home for every holiday, but Connie suspects that he still resents her for her many marriages. She was afraid to lose him then, and she still is. When she met his future wife, Tracy, Connie could see what was in store, and it wasn't pretty.

"The minute I met Tracy, which was about five years before they were married, I knew this was a mistake. But I didn't say a word." A wealthy, beautiful young woman, Tracy seemed to have Mark wound around her little finger. Connie thought she was cold and felt she could not trust her. Sometimes you meet a person and take an instantaneous dislike to him or her. That first reaction is often on the mark, as Malcom Gladwell makes clear in his best-selling book, *Blink*. Connie knew what she had to do.

"I had conceal the fact that I couldn't stand her, or I would lose my son."

When Tracy became pregnant, Connie was determined not to jeopardize her future relationship with her grandchild.

"So I did things like tell her that I loved the way she decorated her house or, when the baby was born, tell her what a wonderful mother she was."

Then, in true *Desperate Housewives* fashion, Tracy began an affair with the husband of Mark's oldest friend from high school. The two couples got divorced, and Tracy married her lover. This left Mark without a wife, without a child, and at odds with his oldest friend (he would not tolerate any criticism of his former wife). To this day, he still won't hear a bad word about Tracy. He expects his mother to get along with Tracy, even though she treated him so badly.

"I've said to Mark that this is the hardest parenting I have ever done, because it's all about keeping quiet." Smiling through the marriage, the courtship, the wedding, and the divorce has been incredibly difficult. Connie puts out maximum effort because she doesn't want to lose her son and granddaughter.

The problem is that Connie now lives thousands of miles away from her daughter-in-law and the baby. Her son could easily pay for the hotel room his mother cannot afford, but he insists that she stay with Tracy in her house. Mark must know what this takes out of his mother. Connie is in a fix: She can't bear to stay with Tracy, so she doesn't see the baby much at all. She has to wait until Tracy sends the baby and the nanny down south to visit. That doesn't happen very often, because Tracy maintains a very tight schedule for her daughter, like most young mothers today. Connie made some real progress when she planned a surprise party for Mark's fortieth birthday.

"I got everybody to come, the whole family, including the baby, and her nanny. I had dreaded calling her for days, but I did it. It was just the way we talked when she was still married to Mark." Connie is proud of having pulled this off, especially because she sees a ray of hope for the future. Mark has a new girlfriend, who is terrific.

Mark has become a much softer and happier man in recent months, and Connie hopes that their relationship will ease, as well. She will never forgive Tracy for the betrayal of Mark, but she will continue to hold her tongue in order to be with the baby. She worries, the way any grandmother would. Handed from nanny to baby-sitter and then back to the nanny, her granddaughter seems to her to be the "poor little rich girl." She says, "I keep thinking Gloria Vanderbilt."

When I ask about the little girl, Connie adds, "She's a ballsy kid, and she is very funny. She got that from her dad. The devil shines from her eyes, so that's very nice."

Every parent knows what it feels like to despise someone who has hurt a beloved child; that anger burns. Connie sees no reason to forgive Tracy or to change her mind about her. She would love to divorce this woman, but she cannot.

"If it weren't for the baby, this would be over. She'd be like my other two ex-husbands—no connection there. But the baby keeps me here."

⁓

Just loving somebody is not a matter of will. But chemistry can be a great ally in one's attempt to keep things going. If there is an instantaneous and strong bond between the newcomer and the original family, life is easier. Sometimes we find natural delight in the company of a relative by marriage.

A Kitten Called Winter

"In a way, I feel fortunate that she is not my daughter."

Carol adored her (third) mother-in-law, and she can't stop loving her stepdaughter, who has been in and out of trouble all her life. Carol believes that the quality of these relationships is due not only to good chemistry but also to the fact that she is not related to them by blood. Good relatives by marriage feel like a gift, and stepchildren in trouble don't stand as a rebuke to your parenting skills. This paradox plays well for Carol, a woman in her mid-sixties, an articulate and accomplished professional. She has been married three times—the third husband seems to be for life. She and her husband, a captain of industry, met at work, and their affair and subsequent marriage created quite a scandal. She adored her third mother-in-law, a warm woman who was naturally affectionate.

"I spoke at her funeral. In the eulogy, I said that I had a profound and uncomplicated love for her. It had no baggage attached to it. It didn't have all the burdens of the past. It was easy for me to love her and easy for her to love me. It was just wonderful." Grief comes in many forms, but two of the most common ones are clear sorrow and messy grief. It is much easier to mourn someone you loved wholeheartedly. The relatives we find most difficult to lay to rest are those who generated mixed feelings in us. The simplicity of Carol's love for her mother-in-law came from their instantaneous connection. This was like manna in the desert for Carol, who comes from a family of Irish Catholics, where you're not supposed to have feelings, much less talk about them. Her mother took this ethic to the extreme.

"At a certain point, I tried to tell my mother that I loved her," Carol tells me.

"She told me she thought such talk was cheap." The only time Carol remembers her mother telling her she loved her was in anger. "If you're my daughter and I love you . . ." It was the most passion she ever showed. Her mother is in her nineties, and Carol takes very good care of her—from afar.

Carol has found that when you marry into a new family you can achieve love uncomplicated by baggage. She also feels simple love for her stepdaughter, who has been on and off serious drugs for the past twenty years. Karen was nine years old when Carol married her father, and she lived with her mother. Unfortunately, when Karen was seventeen, she and her mother moved to San Francisco. She fell into the drug culture there, and she has never really come out of it.

Even though she was a tough kid from the start, Carol was thrilled to have her around. "I loved her. I just loved her. I thought she was wonderful, and I still do."

Carol had always wanted a daughter. At first, Carol had to tell herself, "She is not your daughter." That worked well for both of them when the trouble started. When her mother was fed up with Karen's behavior, she sent her to Carol and her husband. She arrived in her last year of high school and then applied to a local college, and went there. In retrospect, Carol is sure that Karen was using drugs in high school; she was heavily into them in college. Carol's journey from the state of denial to recognition happened when Karen dropped out and moved back to San Francisco. Carol, her husband, and his former wife decided to do an intervention, trying to get Karen into rehab. It didn't work, but in the course of it, Karen's mother took away her key to the apartment—what is called a lockout. Two months later, Karen told her mother she was ready to go into rehab, which she did for nearly a year. But then she landed back on the street. A year later, she called her father collect from a phone booth. "I'm cold" was all she said. Flying to the rescue, Carol and her husband brought her back home. Paradoxically, Carol loved having her live with them.

"She's talented as a visual artist, incredibly verbal, and she writes with incredible clarity and focus. When she is in a good mood, she is the most delightful of companions. There is nobody I'd rather spend time with than Karen. She's witty; she's intelligent; she's sensitive. She's a marvelous person to be with."

Karen started therapy, went back to school, and rescued a white kitten she found beside the road. She named the kitten Winter. Karen took a job at the local bagel shop, stayed in therapy and off drugs, and got her degree. One of her teachers took her aside and told her he thought she was talented and encouraged her to get her B.S. in math and statistics. She did that and landed a wonderful job. But things got rocky when she moved out of the house and into her own apartment. She went back on drugs. Again, her father and stepmother rescued her, again she pulled herself together, and again Carol loved her time with her stepdaughter.

"That week that I spent with her was just the best time I ever had with her—it was so strange. We had such a wonderful time." Carol doesn't think Karen was using while she was with them, and once again Karen agreed to go into rehab.

"We never said the word *drugs* once, because the whole philosophy has changed since the first go-round fifteen years ago. It used to be tough love. Now it's soft love." Karen got out of the facility and moved back to the West Coast, where, to the best of their knowledge, she is holding it together. Nobody expects this to go on forever, but they will be there to pick her up as long as they live.

Carol continues to love Karen as if she were her daughter, but she is also relieved that she is not a blood relative. Carol is not burdened with guilt because she did not raise Karen.

"Her mother has all the pain. Not that I don't have pain with Karen—I do—but I don't have the liabilities of having brought her up, so it's easier for me, somehow. The hard part is when she shuts me out." Of course, she shuts out her parents, too.

If Karen makes it this time, with the help of a kitten called Winter, and the loving support of her natural parents and her stepmother, it will be a miracle. Whatever the future holds, Carol's ability to relate to her stepdaughter without baggage will help the family weather any storm.

It doesn't always work this well. Since a stepparent is new to the family, there are no historical ties to compensate for the tensions caused by small acts of inconsideration. New stepparents may not have patience for the demands of grown kids. These young adults don't look like children to them, and they are not viewed through the lens of memory. One man described his new wife's grown sons as "the mammals," noticing how, when they came home with their friends, they flopped down all over the house. New spouses can feel just as jealous and possessive as grown kids, putting the biological parent in a difficult spot. It is much worse if the grown children didn't approve of the divorce, or are still mourning the death of a parent. As new adults who feel entitled to have a say in their parent's love life (which is not always fair), they have no problem expressing their feelings, loud and clear. To make the situation even more delicate, grown children resent being told what to do by the new relative—even more than they resent advice from the natural parent. Grandchildren are a great boon, because everybody starts that relationship from scratch. But in the early stages of a new marriage, it is sometimes very difficult to preserve the new relationship without breaking up the original family.

Cruel but Not Unusual

Sometimes the children's chemistry with the new parent starts things off on the wrong foot. Esther, a California woman, told me of the instant antipathy her husband's twenty-something daughter had toward her. The daughter had just lost her mother, who had been critically injured in a car accident and died after a long decline. Her father met his new love only a couple of months later, and their chemistry was strong. This romance seemed premature to family and friends, especially to the grieving children. But he had been a dedicated husband and father, especially during the terrible months while his wife was in a coma, and he was very lonely. He also thought that since his kids were in their twenties, they would respond like adults.

They did not approve. They hated Esther on sight, and they took it out on her. She had never married, and had raised no children, so she had no experience to guide her with these grieving young adults. A runner, she got her new husband back into good shape. They speed-walked up and down the hills, often leaving his breathless daughter trying to catch up with them, and fuming in their wake. Esther imagined that she would be getting a family along with her new husband, but that was not the case. One evening, toward the end of a family dinner where she felt the daughter was snubbing her and the son was ignoring her, she retreated to a bedroom and sat there, tears rolling down her cheeks.

"They don't know me well enough to hate me so much."

The daughter went out of her way make it clear that Esther was the enemy. The son and his wife were chilly to the interloper. The father was left with an impossible choice—which he could not and did not make. His children's unabated hostility cast a cloud over the new marriage.

The first grandchild was a big help. The baby adored her grandmother from the moment she was born, and Esther immediately fell in love with the little girl. She would stay with her grandparents on weekends, they would take wonderful outings together, and this child's uncomplicated love began to loosen the tensions in the family. The passage of time also had a soothing effect, and the grown children began to get involved in their own lives and cease the hostilities; Esther, in turn, relaxed and became less sensitive to their slights. She'll never be close to the angry daughter, but no parents are equally close to all their children, step- or otherwise.

Esther believes she had undergone cruel and unusual punishment. Cruel, yes; unusual, no. Stepparents who come on the scene when the children are in their twenties and early thirties are not particularly welcome. It's more difficult if the stepparent never had children. You need to have raised your own kids to translate "I hate you, Mom" into "I have to have the car tonight!"

New stepparents often make the wrong moves, which drives wedges between them and their stepkids. One young woman described a weekend with her father and his second wife. Things had gone relatively well, until the wife called her "my daughter."

"I'm no daughter to her, and I already have a mother," she told me. What she really resented was that her father treated the new wife so much better than he had treated her mother. Nobody knew it, but this new stepmother's effort to create a family when the old one still existed was bound to fail.

It takes incredible patience and self-control to deal with a complicated new family. When there are multiple generations and multiple marriages, the situation begins to resemble three-dimensional tic-tac-toe. It takes more than good chemistry and good character to make things work. Eleanor, the woman in the next story, has two additional strengths: a splendid temperament and the experience of growing up in a big, sprawling family.

You Just Can't Take It Personally

Eleanor, a woman in her middle sixties, has raised a son of her own, divorced her husband and dealt with his new wife, remarried, and found her place in her husband's complex family. This successful corporate executive seems to have a superb emotional GPS. She needs it, with her own son and five grown stepchildren, a former husband and his wife, a new husband and his former wife. She gets along fine with her former husband and his wife, and she has dealt with her son's feelings. When he objected to being with his father and his new wife, she told him, "Listen, this is who your father has chosen. Unless you tell me that she is mean and cruel, you must at least be civil and polite. If you can't manage any more, I understand, and I think your father will, too, but don't you dare be rude to her." Her son respected that point of view, and his stepmother has told other people that she is very appreciative of how Eleanor treats her at family gatherings that include them both.

Eleanor is an old hand with big families. Her brother has six children, and four of them have lived with her at one time or another. After her father died, her mother remarried an old family friend. This marriage lasted twelve years, until he died. Nobody in the family cared for him.

"He tried to be a tyrant to all the children!" said Eleanor. She and her sister and brother tried to keep the cousins in line, while acknowledging their feelings. When they got together for holidays and things became boisterous, this new "grandfather" would take them sternly to task—it was not like the old days. The kids got their revenge one Easter dinner.

"The boys still laugh about this. We were at the dinner table. My sister and her two sons, my son and I, and my mother and her awful husband. He wore a hearing aid. The boys started to whisper during dinner. They'd watch while he'd turn up his hearing aid. Then they'd talk loudly. I about died!" She agreed with the kids' point of view:

"We know how we do family dinners, buddy, so if you're going to be here, you do it our way. This is our house."

Eleanor's second husband has five grown kids. She deals with each of them differently, and she doesn't take their behavior personally. She and her husband fell in love while he was still married (she was divorced, and they met at work). His first wife was furious, and still is; the two daughters sided with their mother. Fifteen years later, the girls never see Eleanor and rarely see their father. Eleanor thinks that it is up to their father to deal with them. The three sons are another story.

She is fine with the eldest, close to the middle son, and she doesn't care at all for the youngest. She appreciates the fact that her eldest stepson is devoted to his father and good to him. Since neither father nor son is a good communicator, Eleanor worked to make more of a connection between them, but she did not go overboard. This peaceful, not intense relationship is a pleasure for everybody.

Her closeness with Greg, the second son, began early in the marriage, long before they spent much time together in person. Their first connection came about when Greg, who was living in Portland, was struggling to decide whether to accept a transfer to Australia, on the other side of the world. He sought Eleanor's advice, and they chatted for hours, forming a warm long-distance relationship. She emphasized the professional advantages of accepting the challenge, but she was also sensitive to the fact that he might be leaving someone important at home. Eleanor says that somehow she always knew Greg was gay, and she made it clear between the lines that this was just fine with her.

"Greg and I bonded on you might say a personal level, because I think Greg knew that I knew what was going on," she says. She also managed to communicate her belief that his father would be all right if he came out—partly because of his personality, and partly because of Eleanor's influence. Years later, when Greg came back from the Antipodes and reunited with his partner, Eleanor and her husband traveled to Portland. Eleanor knew that father and son were apprehensive, but the encounter went well. They both adored Greg's partner. Chemistry played its part. Greg has always been close to his father, and Eleanor feels a special bond with him, largely because of the years when their mutual understanding was warm and unspoken.

She still doesn't like the youngest son, "who is now

thirty-two going on eighteen." Always a problem, always in trouble, always needing money and demanding help from his father, he is hard to take.

"I think he knows that I don't approve of what he does, and that I'm inclined to think in some ways that he is a jerk." And as far as she is concerned, that's okay. He knows Eleanor gets really bent out of shape when he lies to his father. But he will come to her when he thinks there's something she can help him with—advice, for instance. Eleanor engages with him more than with the other sons, but she disapproves of his sneaky ways.

"He's kind of the family beggar. When Greg was doing really well in business and had made a lot of money on the stock of this company, it was fascinating watching his younger brother try to go after it." Eleanor, ever the wise woman, held her tongue.

She doesn't really care what this stepson and his girl-friend think of her, but she's a protective she-bear around her husband.

Every story in this chapter, except for Peggy's, could have ended badly. Each of the families could have been torn apart by the problems they encountered. It takes determination to go the distance in any family; complicated families can be much more demanding. Maybe keeping a complicated family together is like swimming laps: dive in, stroke, stroke, and breathe. Keep going. Sometimes you have to rotate your body to cut through the water cleanly.

Sometimes you think that you will never catch your breath again. But you keep on breathing and kicking, and you keep on stroking. Eventually, the effort seems less exhausting. At the end of the swim, you have new strength, and the desire to dive in again.

6

IT's A GIRL!

No matter what the family dynamic was before, the world changes when the first grandchild is born. When people joke that they are too young to be grandparents, they are paying heed to the generational shift. We begin to imagine ourselves living long enough to attend their graduations, weddings, and the birth of their children. When we realize that our grandchildren will be living another eighty or ninety years, the future becomes more real. Grandchildren offer the additional benefit of slowing down our sense of aging, because they grow up so much faster than we grow old. Watching them in their family gives us the opportunity to reconnect with the years when we were young parents, just as raising our children allowed us to revisit our own childhoods. I remember realizing, when I had my first child, that I could undo the mistakes I thought my parents had made with me. Like most people, I raised my children in light of what I remembered about what I liked and didn't like—doing the same or the opposite, depending on the situation.

Watching the grandkids and dealing with their parents gives us another shot at getting things right, because, of course, we remember the mistakes we made with our kids, and so do they. So it's fascinating—and somewhat daunting—to see our children correcting what they didn't like about their childhoods. A young father who was raised in a family that fought and screamed will not allow such behavior in his home once he has kids. A woman who grew up in a family of psychiatrists banned all psychobabble from her family table when she had children. Sometimes we can even catch our children repeating what they enjoyed, and it feels wonderful. A new father planned a family vacation just like the ones he took with his parents—to their quiet delight. Sometimes you can hear a child singing a lullaby that you sang to her when she was a baby; family rituals that take shape in the new household may look suspiciously like ones you handed down from your parents. The arrival of grandchildren gives us two-way vision. We can watch the new family and look back at the old one.

Many people tell me how much they treasure the fact that they can be better grandparents than they were parents. Now they are not so busy, so engaged in their own lives and careers; most don't have to take care of the grandchildren when they feel exhausted and grumpy; their patience for these young creatures is much greater than it was for their own children.

~~

The style of parenting that we observe our children practicing may feel like a judgment on us, and that's painful. Changing times and child-rearing views can feel like attacks. If it was good enough for you, it's good enough for your baby, we can't help thinking. So arguments about everything, from food (sweets are out; avocados are in), to discipline, to television, become personal and painful. And when the parents of our grandchildren seem ready to judge us at every turn, it's awful.

The best way to handle this is to heed the eleventh commandment: Thou shalt not give your grown children advice. But there is a corollary to that ban on criticism. We can support the new parents in every imaginable way, not necessarily with time and money, but with a recognition that babies and small children are hard to raise, exhausting, and sometimes scary. If we can remember how hard it was for us when our children were little, we can comfort a nervous new parent with a sympathetic word or a small kindness. This is different from approving everything they do. But the act of retroactive empathy goes a long way toward encouraging the young parents. Not only do they feel less at sea but they come back for more.

Since the parents control access to the grandchildren, and we want to be with them, we need to make sure that we're getting along well with both new parents. Mothers of sons have the task of making sure they get along with their daughters-in-law, and mothers of daughters need to figure out what their daughters want and how to meet their needs.

Stopped at the Gates

The family table is already set when the baby arrives, and the existing relationships between parents and their grown children, both within the nuclear family and with the in-laws, have an enormous impact.

Patricia is a smart, witty, good-looking woman with six grandchildren, four boys and two girls. A government official, she lives in the Washington, D.C. area. Her two sons live nearby. She has always been closer to her younger son, and things with the older son have always been tense, ever since he was a child. This difference played out when both of her sons became fathers, a year apart. The arrival of the elder son's baby was a train wreck for the family, although the newborn was fine.

Patricia and her husband had been told that their first son's wife was in labor, and since the hospital was not far away, they waited at home, as requested. When they could no longer bear the suspense, they drove to the hospital, wanting to be there when the baby arrived. Patricia was nervous and scared—the labor was taking a long time—and she asked for information about the progress of the labor and the health of mother and baby. Unfortunately, the new privacy rules mandate that the hospital cannot give out such information. This didn't stop Patricia from inquiring again—after all, this was her first grandchild—but it was to no avail. Their son was in the birthing room with his wife, and so they had no source of information. Their anxiety mounted. Then their son stormed into the waiting room and informed them that the doctor had just told his wife that a psychotic grandmother was making trouble downstairs. The couple was furious at Patricia, who has walked on eggshells with that family ever since.

A year later, her younger son's first child was born. What a difference. The labor was not as difficult and did not last so long. Patricia and her husband sat in the same hospital, waiting together with their daughter-in-law's parents. At some point, all four of them crept toward the door of the birthing room, trying to catch a glimpse from within. When Patricia's son came out to give them the good news, they all toppled through the door together. The door to this son's home has never been closed to Patricia. Even though this family now lives across the country, they are still close.

The pattern of these interactions continues: The degree of coolness or closeness with each son sets the stage for what happens with each son's wife and with the grandchildren. To this day, the first son and his wife don't let their kids go out alone with Patricia and her husband. The eldest child is now six. When Patricia offered to take him to the Air and Space Museum, she was told, "You might lose him." She had never lost a child anywhere, but she worries that she is losing her son and his wife and access to their children. The grandchildren have picked up their parents' signals. Last summer, they were at the shore. Patricia took her grandson's hand and said, "Let's go shell hunting." As they approached the ocean's edge, she began pointing out the interesting shells. The little boy paused, looked back, and then said, "I think I'd better go be with Mommy."

<hr />

Patricia's problems with her first son and his wife have a long history. Years before, Patricia was talking on the phone to this son when he was also in the middle of a big fight with his future wife. They were screaming at each other. Overhearing the angry words, Patricia said, "I shouldn't be hearing this. So I'm going to hang up now."

A month later, the family was out for dinner, and her son announced their engagement. Patricia couldn't control herself. The look on her face when she heard this news was not lost on her son and his fiancée. Patricia acknowledges that this was not the way to begin a wonderful relationship with her daughter-in-law. She is right.

Things have never been easy with her son, and she has never gotten close to his wife—she's not someone Patricia would naturally warm to, although she admires much about her and tells me she has come through like a pro in times of crisis. Patricia appreciates this in her son's wife. She realizes that she will never get to take these grandchildren anywhere until she clears things up with her son.

That's where the problem lies, she knows. Recently some-body told Patricia that Wolf Blitzer, the CNN correspond-ent, calls his mother twice a day from wherever he is in the world.

She mentioned this to her son, and they both laughed. That was the closest she has come to discussing their rela-tionship, she tells me.

"I've been thinking of telling him, 'I'm sorry for the mistakes I made when you were growing up. I did the best could, and I love you. Can't we bury the hatchet?' "

"Why don't you?"

"Because I'm afraid of the response."

When she heard that I have found deep love and grat-itude in even the most irritable and testy grown children, she perked up. Later that day, I got a message from her, telling me that she had called her daughter-in-law just to chat, and they both enjoyed the conversation. She was thinking that she might have a real talk with her son now, too.

Acknowledging mistakes and having an honest conver-sation about the past make a big difference. Many people are afraid of such an encounter. Others are so angry and hurt that they don't think they could control their tem-pers. Few people have the courage to bring up problems like this with their grown kids. Most of us are content to live with the wall of silence that keeps conflict at bay. The problem is that this wall also keeps intimacy away—and honesty. Anger and guilt are a toxic combination, and who wants to expose them? I guess the question is, What will you go through to be close to your grandchildren?

If controlling access to the grandchildren is a powerful weapon our grown children have, wanting to be with them offers us a powerful incentive to take on the difficult issues. The desire to experience the pleasure of the little ones can make a grandmother see virtues she never noticed in her daughter-in-law, and strengths she never saw in her son. But some parents have a very hard time making peace with the new generation, and it is painful to watch what happens.

Losers, Weepers

"It's not my mommy."

Sara is lovely; her round, open face breaks into a smile that warms your spirit. Today, she has short hair and a big belly—her second child is due any minute. She's smart and direct, but very kind. She and her husband, Alan, both thirty-six, have been together for a decade. They live in St. Louis with their two-year-old daughter. I have been told that if you are looking for a role model for a mother of a small child, go to Sara.

From the first time she met Alan's mother, Nettie, Sara felt that something was off. As the young couple pulled up to his parents' house and Sara got out of the car, a woman opened the front door and came out to greet her. Sara thought she was meeting Alan's mother, but she was mistaken. Nettie had asked a girlfriend to greet Sara so she could have a good peek at the girl from behind the window curtains. Sara was disconcerted, set off balance, and she has felt that way ever since. She gradually discovered that she could never get it right with Nettie. If she offered to clear the table, she was told, "No, no, no. Sit, I'll do it." If she didn't get up, Nettie would say, "I hope you're enjoying your relaxing time here. Don't worry. I can do it myself."

Nettie cannot help herself. For instance, she took to calling Sara "Fatty" when she was was pregnant, which hurt Sara's feelings.

She adores her two sons; they mean everything to her—everything. She needs to be exceedingly close to them. She finds it almost impossible to observe the boundaries that grown children require. When she baby-sat for her first grandchild, she didn't see anything wrong with rearranging her daughter-in-law's pantry—the old pasta was just on the verge of getting moldy. She didn't see anything wrong with giving presents to the nanny, even though her son and daughter-in-law asked her not to. She butted into many aspects of their lives.

You can sympathize with Nettie's bumbling efforts to form a relationship with her daughter-in-law, but you can also sense her ambivalence about the newcomer to the family. She only wants the best for her son, so she is always interfering. She heard that they were going away for the weekend and inquired about where they were staying, and what it cost. Then she thought it over and called back two hours later. "Listen, I made you a reservation at this other place. You don't have to go, but it's a hundred and seventy-five dollars, and that includes breakfast. And I heard the place you booked is not good," she said. Once, Sara's husband and his mother got into such a fight over her meddling that Nettie, in a rage, said, "You're not my son anymore."

Sara seethed with anger. She comforted herself by re-membering that Nettie was her husband's problem. Weeks after each set-to, Nettie would apologize, call herself ter-rible names, and promise never to do it again. Alan loves his mother and would agree to try again. Sara thinks that apologies ring hollow if they are not accompanied by changes in behavior.

Nettie wanted to be the perfect grandmother when the first baby was born. But she couldn't control her need to make things perfect—as she saw perfect. So when the ques-tion of a pacifier came up, her anxiety at the parents' in-decision mounted. She kept calling with advice, first from her friends, then from the Internet, and finally from books she took out of the library. That may be loving be-havior, but it is infuriating. Sara reddens with anger as she continues the story of Grandma Nettie.

Sara invited her in-laws to spend one day a week with their little girl. It was great for the little girl, and it gave the nanny a day off, but Nettie was soon meddling in their home, stepping over the boundaries with her daughter-in-law. Even though these visits made her tense, Sara rec-ognized the importance of grandparents' involvement in a child's life, and she knew how much it mattered to her husband.

When she came home from work, the baby would cry for her, so Sara would slip upstairs, in deference to her in-laws' feelings. She knew the baby would settle down the minute she was out of sight. She didn't realize how hard this was on the grandparents. One day, Nettie couldn't take it any longer. She invited her daughter-in-law to lunch.

Sara said okay, and they chose a day when she'd be working from home, so they could eat in the neighborhood. After a pleasant beginning, the lunch turned into a griping session, on both sides. Sara said what was on her mind: She didn't like having her home reorganized, and she did not appreciate her mother-in-law's habit of buying presents for the nanny. Sara, after all, was in charge of her kitchen and her housekeeper. When Nettie objected, Sara was annoyed.

"Stop buying things. Just stop doing that. I will handle it in whatever way I want," she told Nettie. Then what had started out as a healthy airing of grievances degenerated into all-out war.

"Sara," Nettie said, "you're not giving the baby what she needs. That's why we've been around so much. If you've noticed, we haven't gone to Florida at all. I feel like I need to be around, because something's obviously going wrong. And I've noticed when you come home from work, you don't go over to the baby and pick her up." Then came a detailed list of all the things Nettie believed Sara had done wrong.

"Remember that time . . . Remember that time . . ."

"The baby cries a lot, but not around us—only around you," said Nettie. Sara was incredulous.

"We know something is wrong. We want to help.

Wouldn't you ask for help if you needed it?" Then came Nettie's pièce de résistance: "You're just not devoted to her."

"You're are telling me that the minute I get home, I should be totally focused on the child?"

"Yes."

Sara felt like a deer caught in the headlights. She shakes her head as she tells the story.

"I wish I had picked up my water glass and thrown it in her face," she says.

Nettie had gone too far, and the reverberations from this lunch lasted a long time. The young couple spent the weekend talking and crying. Alan confessed that his mother had confided all this to him the week before. He had begged her not to speak her mind to Sara. Sara appreciated his efforts, but she had reached her limit.

"Here's the thing, Alan. I want to support you, but I need you to understand that my relationship with them is now permanently over. It'll be easy for me. I don't care about them, but I understand these are your parents."

Unfortunately, the fight didn't stop there. The next week, denied access to her son's home and baby, Nettie started calling Alan at his office. When he didn't respond, she started leaving threatening voice mails.

"I know what's going on up there. I will call Child Services if I need to." Sara and Alan work a half hour from home, so they ended up changing the locks on their house, to keep Nettie out. At one point, the threats were so severe that Sara called her neighbor and asked her to pick up the baby and the nanny.

Nettie never called Child Protective Services. This outburst was just one of her out-of-control moments. The two families didn't speak for months. Alan persuaded his mother to go into family therapy with him. Sara comforts herself by saying, "These are his parents. I don't have to deal with them. It's not my mommy."

Alan takes their daughter to see his parents every week, but they no longer spend the day with their granddaughter. Sara has given up on Nettie. Even though she knows she is a good mother, Sara has suffered a loss of confidence. Recently, she counseled a friend who is also dealing with an interfering mother-in-law. "Try to come away from your conversations with her," said Sara, "in a way that preserves your own sense of self and your own sense of dignity."

Nettie was just trying to help. She has a strong opinion about every detail of her son's life; she can't keep from interfering. Nettie is not stupid; she knows she has ruined her relationship with her daughter-in-law, as her apologies to Alan and her willingness to go to family therapy with her son attest. She's just not in control. Everybody in this family has lost something. Sara, whose father was a Holocaust survivor and lost his entire family in the war, is losing Alan's family. Alan, who recognizes that his mother can be a pain in the neck, has lost the opportunity to enjoy his whole family together. The biggest losers are the two grandparents, who see their grandchild only under strained circumstances, and who know they may never get their son back completely.

Mothers of sons understand that, in our culture, the

mother-daughter tie is the stronger one. They know they are in danger of losing their sons—and the grandchildren—to the wife's family. So mothers of sons need to strengthen the bond with their daughters-in-law. Mothers of daughters have it easier, as the next stories attest. But there is more to this than the gender of the grown child. In Carolyn's story, the ease of the present was set up over half a century ago.

War Babies

Carolyn, a New England woman in her sixties, grew up in an extremely loving home amid an extended family. A little girl during World War II, she, her mother, and her brother lived with her mother's parents, along with the aunts and cousins, whose men were also off fighting.

"Talking to you, I am thinking about how close we were," she says. "I was real little, but I remember spending lots of time with my grandparents." She adored them.

Like most people of that generation, they were very strict. She had rules to follow, but her grandparents were always loving and supportive.

"Not that we didn't have our teenage years, but I always felt I had a secure and safe place to go, where I did not experience criticism." Carolyn's paternal grandparents had died before she was born, but her family spent summer vacations with relatives in their hometown, which cemented her strong ties with her father's side of the family.

Family sustained Carolyn when her husband died and

her two children were small. She went to work full-time to support them. Perhaps because of this, she has always been close to her children. After they grew up and married, Carolyn's mother began to fail. Instead of commuting every weekend to take care of her, Carolyn moved back to the town where she grew up—and where her mother still lived.

"I've never regretted it, because I had ten years with her." Her brother, who had been in the military, decided to move back home around the same time. "We're very close because it's just the two of us."

A couple of years ago, to Carolyn's delight, her daughter Amanda, Amanda's husband, and their teenage daughter chose to move back home to live with her. Amanda's husband was being transferred to a town nearby. The three of them get along very well and have divided up daily tasks in an interesting way. Carolyn has a responsible job in town, and her son-in-law is pursuing his career. Amanda stays home, cares for the household, and is there when her teenage daughter comes home from school. Carolyn has ceded control of many aspects of her home, especially the kitchen.

"You have to be willing to give up some things," she says. Amanda is a terrific cook, which is a relief, because Carolyn was a lousy cook, by her own admission, famous for her "cowpat cake."

In return for giving up control, Carolyn gets to spend lots of time with her granddaughter. She loves being with this young teenager. Even with her job, Carolyn has more time for her than she had for her own children, because as a single mom working full-time and raising two children, she was always exhausted.

"I just love having time with my firstborn granddaughter. We will spend a whole day together going to the movies and shopping. That is something I can do now. I think it's great for the parents, too, because they get some time alone together." Carolyn instinctively knows to stay out of disputes between Amanda and her daughter. Sometimes she'll suggest strategies to her granddaughter, but she will not get into the middle of their disagreements.

"If my daughter wants to discuss it with me, we discuss it. But it's her daughter, not mine, and she has to make those decisions. I do not interfere. If they're having an argument about what kind of clothes she is going to wear to school, if her dress is too short, I never offer an opinion." At first, the teenager tried to manipulate her grandmother into taking her side, but she soon realized that Carolyn was not playing.

"I just try to get her to strategize. When we go out to eat or go to a movie, I'll say, 'I know it's very tough for you, but maybe you should try this. Think positive on this. Be smart about this. It's about how you handle things.' " She doesn't get into "Your mom did this," or "You did that." She just talks about ways to get through life. What a lucky girl. She has the best kind of life coach, her grandmother. Carolyn gives me a sense of how she spends her weekends.

"This weekend, we have a Christmas parade in town, so we are all involved helping decorate the float for the Congregational church. Friday night, I am eating with my good friends. Saturday, I've already said to my daughter and son-in-law that they need to get out and do something, because my granddaughter and I have plans. Actually, Saturday I am having lunch with friends, and then in the evening I'll baby-sit. Sunday we'll have breakfast together and be out getting ready for the holiday parade."

Carolyn is content. She doesn't know if this arrangement is permanent, because her son-in-law's job may take him elsewhere. She has made it clear that she's going to be fine, whatever happens. But she is enjoying every minute of this family closeness, and she tells me that her brother has had the same good luck: About a year ago, his second daughter and her family moved back home and are living with him—just around the corner from Carolyn and her family.

How do we understand the differences among the experiences of the three grandmothers we have just met? Of course, mothers of sons often have to shore up two relationships, where mothers of daughters can often rely on the closeness of the bond they have with their daughters. Personality style is important. Patricia is intense and sharp, Nettie is controlling and can't keep her mouth shut, and Carolyn is low-key. Another factor is the difference in the grandmothers' marital status. Patricia and her husband, and Nettie and her husband, have been married forever. Carolyn was widowed in her thirties, and her situation naturally drew her close to her kids.

It's also important to take a look at what the grandparents want from their kids. For Patricia, living in the same house with either of her sons and their families would be a version of Dante's *Inferno*. Nettie wants her son back, in the old relationship, where she could make him do what she thinks is best for him. Carolyn cherishes the closeness with her family, in part because she spent her childhood embraced by her big family, and in part because she felt so alone after her husband died.

It is not only war that casts a shadow over families. So do social movements and social unrest. The placid fifties gave the conformist message to many families. The sixties had a tremendous impact on parents of our generation, when sex and drugs and rock and roll combined to make rebels of us all.

Love Story

"My job as a grandmother is to back off from giving advice and work on giving praise."

This is a love story—about three women, and four generations. Linda is a pretty woman in her fifties, whose long curly blondish hair forms a nimbus around her head and her shoulders. She plays with a lock of hair as she talks. The signs of her youth as a hippie are everywhere, from the dangling jewelry, to the ruffled jeans, to the colorful patterned coat she wraps around herself. Her face is weathered, from the sun and from life, and her voice is buttery and warm.

She has been through a lot. Linda was divorced soon after her daughter was born, and because she was quite ill with a then-undiagnosed disease (chronic fatigue syndrome), she had a hard time making enough money to support her daughter and herself (she was a musician). She took care of her daughter as best she could. A struggling artist, Linda was not naturally maternal, she admits in retrospect. But she didn't dare share custody with her former husband, because he had married a woman who was not kind to her husband's little girl.

Mother and daughter had a rocky relationship when she was a teenager, especially when she got into drugs. Then, when this girl was in her twenties and working as a bartender, she found herself pregnant. She didn't want to marry the father, immediately took herself off all dangerous substances, and struggled with whether or not to have the baby. She moved in with Linda, who was able to keep her opinions to herself. Though it was not easy, she never said what she favored at the time. She explained that she would support her daughter whatever she decided. Her daughter decided to have the baby.

Linda was in the birthing room when the baby was born. Looking around the crowded room, Linda decided to step back and leave it to the experts, and in that moment, she discovered the first rule of grandparenthood: "The grandmother is an advisory position. I think a lot of women don't get that. If they could understand it, they'd be so much happier." The labor was short and intense, and Linda's daughter was fully conscious. Linda cut the umbilical cord.

"I had a few minutes with the baby after, and I swear she looked right at me. I have a deep connection with this baby. Right now if you come to my home, it's a home of people who are all in love with one another. My little girl is such a good mother. She's much more relaxed than I ever was."

Linda remembers being a nervous mother. She was sick, raising her daughter on her own, and her own upbringing hadn't been easy. She had a brilliant perfectionist for a mother, a person who would sooner break off a relationship permanently than negotiate to preserve it. Her father, now in his eighties, is often abrasive.

"He can offer something and then take it away. He can say horrible things. I have published a book [now she's a writer], and he still doesn't see me as a viable human being, because I am a female. Still I love him, and he is welcome in my home. In fact, he feels very happy in my home."

While Linda is nonjudgmental with her daughter, she sets limits with her father, who spends one week a month with them.

"Does he behave himself?" I ask.

"I make him." Linda has discovered how to adjust the atmosphere in her home. Linda feels good about her newfound power.

"I am the matriarch. I am the head of the household.

That gives me the power to set the tone in my home."
When I ask Linda how she turned the corner with her father, she tells me, "A lifetime of spiritual practice has made it possible for me to love my father as he is."

The baby is now six months old. They all are beginning to sleep through the night, and the laundry no longer forms a high pile in the living room. Linda has slipped into the grandmother role with ease.

"She is the mom, so she's going to make all the decisions about her baby. Because we have such a good relationship, I have my cache of influence. And also it is a problem if you think you can bully your adult child into behaving."

Some people are able to turn themselves away from the harshness of their childhood. Linda has taken on three generations at the same time, finding the strength to let her child be the mother she wants to be, without interference, and to keep her father in bounds, so she doesn't have to exile him. Linda has succeeded in correcting the mistakes she made with her daughter, working out a new relationship with her father, and gathering all the generations together in her home. It's quite an accomplishment. She credits her spiritual practice. I credit Linda for doing that, too. Everybody needs a source of strength that comes from something beyond themselves.

Singing the Blues

*"I was the kind of person who just woke up sad every day.
I've been sad for a long time."*

It is hard to be fifty years old and raising a difficult little boy of four. Grandparents all over the world are doing this. Listening to Laura trying to take it in stride, while being honest about her feelings, is painful.

Laura sings with a small group of musicians who entertain in their town. Her voice is like an antique pearl, smooth and warm. Her gorgeous white hair is cut geometrically, setting off her beautiful face and accentuating her gray eyes. The sadness that radiates from Laura is free of self-pity. She is in a hard place. Laura traveled the country when she was young, leaving her two daughters (each by a different husband) when she toured. Now she teaches violin. Her elder daughter has a good job and is making a life for herself; they are very close.

Laura's sadness is about her younger daughter, Paula. Gifted in so many ways, Paula became a serious problem once she hit the teen years: She used drugs and stole not only from her parents but also from her big sister. Laura's guilt for leaving Paula when she went on tour intensifies her sadness.

Paula got pregnant at sixteen. Not long after, she descended into psychosis, and now she lives in a psychiatric hospital. Laura has finally come to accept the fact that Paula has a chemical imbalance. She and her husband made Paula a ward of the state when their insurance coverage ran out. Paula's hallucinations make her believe that she is God and her little boy, Tyler, is the Messiah. She told one of the aides in the hospital that she would sacrifice her son's life if God commanded her to.

"We feel we have to protect him from her," Laura says, "even though she hasn't done anything overt around him so far."

The little boy's father, also highly gifted, is in jail for assault. Both he and Paula were taking drugs during Paula's pregnancy. At first, Paula insisted on trying to take care of Tyler herself. She was in a home for pregnant girls and young mothers right before he was born, and they lived there for the first year of his life. When Paula moved into a setting that gave her more independence, she showed poor judgment caring for the baby, and the authorities were prepared to take Tyler away from her.

Laura got Tyler when he was just over a year old. "So, he's been at our house ever since," she says.

He has a high IQ, and at age four reads, plays piano, and does elementary arithmetic by himself. Otherwise, he is glued to the TV or the computer. He is very hard to discipline, and he gets very upset when his routine is disrupted.

"I think he wants to please us for the most part, but he also doesn't like to be told what to do. At school, he will pitch a fit over not being first in line, and he flies into rages at other children. He wants everything his way."

Laura tries to reason with him. "Okay, you can make a scene but it's not going to change anything. Do you really want to go through all this?" Sometimes he will go along with her. But at other times, this conversation doesn't work, and Laura has to be a disciplinarian.

"I hate it. I don't like to be firm; I don't like to be mean. I just like for everybody to be happy." Tyler may be difficult, or autistic, or his brain may have been damaged by the drugs his mother was taking before he was born.

Laura keeps Tyler away from his mother, out of necessity, and she has legally adopted him. A cousin told Tyler that Paula is his birth mother, and Laura expects Tyler to resent her for this separation when he grows up. When he has been with his mother, the connection is immediate and powerful. Tyler misses her.

"Getting up in the morning isn't just getting up and drinking coffee," says Laura, describing her day. "It's getting up and making sure he's gotten his bath, changed his underpants, and has had his cereal." She or her husband takes him to day care and then Laura fits in her music lessons around Tyler's schedule. Laura's husband does as much as he can, but the primary burden is on her.

"Then we fight over dinner, the bath, bedtime stories, and so on.

"Actually, that's one of the bigger things I hadn't remembered about raising children—just having to be aware of where they are all the time. To go out for a night last Saturday, I spent thirty-five dollars on a baby-sitter! If you want to do something, you have to plan around him."

Laura not only feels guilty for Paula's troubles, and Tyler's; she judges herself by the standard her mother set.

"My mom embodies the serenity prayer. If she can't fix something, she won't worry about it. She'll take what comes her way and doesn't complain. That's where I'm different. I can't just go, 'Okay, I'll just make the most of it and be happy.' "

Laura is sacrificing her middle age to raise her grandson, and she doesn't have much hope for the future. There is not a lot of family left, and, as she says, "I will be dead before he is my age." She may not be the saint her mother is, but she is taking it day by day and trying to enjoy the little things.

"I enjoy gardening a whole lot. I enjoy music a lot. It sounds funny, but for a while there I was too sad to enjoy anything. It was as if my sorrow was making me cut off my nose to spite my face. Now, I've given myself permission to enjoy what I can."

I look across the table at this lovely woman, and I wonder how she can face the endless prospect of dealing with a mentally ill daughter and raising a difficult child. Laura has a philosophy that helps her survive: "Nobody lives a life without some problems. Life has sad things in it. People lose their children. I am trying to see it in a broader picture. I sure have empathy for other people who go through these things." Laura's empathy for others is an important part of her makeup. If only she could extend that forgiveness to herself.

†⌣†

I am struck by the powerful choices we are given at this point in our lives, and how our decisions will affect our future, and that of our children. Of course, nothing is entirely in our control. Geography, for instance, is a terrible thing for grandparents who live thousands of miles away from their grandkids. A woman I know was telling me that her daughter and her family eat most dinners at her in-laws', who live nearby; she's thoroughly jealous of this closeness, but she knows what a great help the in-laws are. Instead of worrying about her comparative closeness with her granddaughter, she's planning a weeklong vacation, so that she and her husband can bond with the baby.

We have to adjust; we have to be supple. If we feel that we are doing all the heavy lifting, so be it. So much depends on our relationship with our grown children. If we don't get along, there's not much likelihood of being close to the next generation. On the other hand, clearing the air with our grown children and their spouses has its own advantages, so this effort can do double duty.

So many people remember their grandparents with love and admiration, and they still miss them. Loving grandparents leave a precious legacy. When we tell our grandchildren stories about our grandparents, they are fascinated. They love to hear about how people lived so very long ago. Their eyes open wide when we tell them that we actually knew people who were born in the nineteenth century.

Think of that.

If we put in the time and effort with our children and their kids, creating that special bond across the generations, our grandkids will tell their grandchildren all about us. They will tell them stories about what we were like, and how we lived. They will get from their grandchildren the same amazed look when they tell them that we were born in the twentieth century.

Think of that.

7

THE ROOT OF ALL EVIL

The money that pays for life's necessities is often called "cold hard cash." It serves a critical function, and when there isn't enough to feed and clothe and educate our families, money can rule our lives. Discretionary money, especially when it moves between generations, takes on other attributes according to relationships, history, and character.

Discretionary money represents control, guilt, an emotional debt from the past, and a symbol of favoritism among siblings. It is a chameleon, taking on different colors at different times in every family situation. This is what lends it tremendous emotional and moral significance.

><-

I know a man whose mother cut his brother out of her will because she never forgave him for marrying the wrong woman. The day her will was read, the brother aged ten years. She had cut him off with these words: "To my son George, for reasons he understands, I leave nothing." She was a difficult woman, and nobody much cared for her, but I kept imagining this woman's hand rising from the grave and slapping her son across the face. It was then that I learned the power of money to wound. That woman never wavered from the threat she made decades before her death. One thing can be said about her: She meant what she said.

When my friend's father died, his will left it up to her and her brother to divide the estate equitably, based on jointly calculating who had received what when their parents were alive. This brother and sister could not bear the Solomonic burden of their father's will. Arguments over what was fair brought up a lifetime of competition and much anger. They were estranged for ten years. Hearing this story, I understood the power of money to divide.

The wish implicit in this man's will was that brother and sister should get closer after he died. He should have known that the effort to manipulate your children's relationship never works, whether you are alive or dead. At the end of life the money issues often become terrible, but there is plenty we can do to avoid leaving lasting scars on our descendants. We have to start early.

Money issues should start being dealt with long before the deathbed. The day-to-day interactions concerning money in a family begin with discussions of allowances and continue throughout our lives. Some parents believe that they should be absolutely evenhanded with their children, giving whatever they have to each equally. Others take a more socialist view: to each according to her need. Arguments between husband and wife ensue; both theories are right and wrong. If you pay tuition for a daughter and not for a son, does your son deserve a gift in kind? If you pay medical expenses for one couple, does the other get the same amount of help, even if they don't need it? To complicate things, couples disagree on these matters. One parent knows for certain that scarves and mittens are appropriate holiday gifts for a grown child, and the other believes a lavish gift is warranted. Which is right: gloves or a car? When should we stop picking up the dinner bill? How do we feel about asking them for help? How do we tell them we can't help them because we don't have enough for ourselves? Nobody wants to talk about money with grown children, but if you don't, it can be the elephant in the room.

Today, many members of the baby-boom generation are better off than their children, and acts of generosity are common. In the July 14, 2005, issue of the *New York Times,* Tamar Lewin reported that many Manhattan grandparents are paying for their grandchildren's private schools, camp, and vacations because they can afford these expenses and their adult children cannot. Lewin stated that most of the people she interviewed who receive help from their parents didn't want to be identified in the article. They are ambivalent about taking the money. They are grateful to their parents, but embarrassed that they need help, and extremely sensitive to the issue of control. Lewin did not write about the parents who help their children financially but are resentful of their demands.

Needy but Nice

Evelyn and her daughter, Denise, forty-three, ought to get along very well. They love to gossip; they enjoy the same movies and books; they adore Denise's children. Given the choice of chatting with her daughter or a friend her own age, Evelyn would choose Denise. But an under-current of mistrust and anger eats away at their relation-ship. Evelyn cannot forgive Denise for asking for money and has always resented giving it to her. Denise interprets her mother's tightfistedness as a lack of love and sup-port. Evelyn thinks that Denise's need for financial help from her is a sign of immaturity and dependence. Denise, knowing that her mother can afford it, cannot fathom why she is so stingy. Evelyn married badly, twice. Her first hus-band, Denise's father, couldn't hold a job for long, and her second husband, the father of her second child, a boy, left them before mother and son could check out of the hospital.

Denise was an adolescent when her baby brother was

born. The family moved from the city to the suburbs, and she was taken out of a private school she loved and enrolled in a large public middle school. This once-terrific student suddenly lost interest in her studies. Evelyn did not see that all these changes—a new baby, a new neighborhood, and a new school—might have played a role in Denise's decline: She dropped out of high school and it took years until she got her GED. This made her brilliant and academically accomplished mother furious. Denise eventually went to college and did well, but, much to her mother's disappointment, she refused to apply to medical school, even though she excelled in the sciences.

To make matters worse, Denise chose to work in the nonprofit sector, which pays poorly. Denise married very young, but her husband (and the father of her children) left her when the kids were small and pays no child support.

She has asked her mother for money ever since college. According to Evelyn, she has always needed more than seems appropriate. A single mother, Denise has been unable to support her two children. Her choice of idealistic and low-paying jobs drives Evelyn to distraction. She feels that her daughter is constantly manipulating her. She does not want to help Denise, but when the mortgage is due or the cupboard is bare, what's a mother to do?

Her son was always an easy child. He and his mother get along well, and they did so from the time he was little. An outstanding student like his mother, and a good money manager, he is engaged to a lovely young woman, and his prospects are bright. Benjamin lived at home with

Evelyn for a number of years after college and graduate school, and during that time saved the money he would have spent on living expenses. Evelyn does not consider the years he lived rent-free as a contribution from her. He never asked for money.

Evelyn, a successful a lawyer, made a fine living. Her house, in a good neighborhood in Chicago, is very large and worth a fortune on today's market. Now she is retired, and although she is well-off, she no longer feels wealthy. She resents Denise's incessant requests for money even more now and believes that her daughter's financial dependence is a character defect.

Evelyn's view is somewhat unrealistic. This is what happened the year after Denise graduated from college. Evelyn invited her daughter, who was living in California, to meet her and the little brother in Colorado for a week of skiing. This sounded great to Denise. She was ready to go. Then Evelyn added, "I'll pay your skiing fees."

"What? You're going to make me pay for everything else?" asked Denise, who was in her first (nonprofit) job and could not possibly afford the plane fare and hotel costs.

"I can't go unless you pay," she told her mother. Evelyn was outraged; she thought, There she goes again, being grabby. She did not think it was odd that she gave the boy a free ride but did not do the same for Denise.

"Once you graduate from college," she told me, "you shouldn't ask your parents for financial help." Evelyn correctly interpreted the look on my face: It was a frown.

"Do you think I did the wrong thing?" she asked. I nodded.

"I do, too," she said. As I started telling Evelyn how many people in their twenties still rely on their parents, especially for fun things like ski trips, Evelyn interrupted me.

"I mean I was wrong to pay her way, which is what I did. She guilted me into it." I was thinking that Evelyn was wrong to refuse to pay her daughter's airfare and hotel in the first place.

Over the years, Denise has talked Evelyn into helping her with the down payment on her house, the mortgage, her credit-card bills, and things for her children. She shades her requests in many guises, from SOS messages to hints about how much the kids would like camp. Evelyn feels that her daughter is manipulating her every time she calls, even to chat. The decades of resentment on both sides have created a perpetual state of anger and mistrust. Evelyn keeps the accounts in her head. Denise is always in the red; Benjamin is always in the black.

Recently, Denise left the nonprofit sector and took a job in private industry. For the first time, her salary should cover all her expenses. Evelyn is thrilled. But she does not know whether Denise's financial independence will help her forgive her daughter for cadging money over the years. And she thinks Denise will never be properly appreciative of what she has been given.

Evelyn wants to heal the breach between them, and perhaps Denise's efforts to support herself will improve their relationship. That's the good news. The bad news is that the misinterpretations and harsh judgments that dog their interactions around money spill over into everything else. But even selfless generosity, which didn't happen here, carries heavy emotional baggage, I discovered.

Caught in the Net

Elizabeth's mother has always been happy to help her daughter out. She shares office space in her apartment (they are both therapists); she runs down to Elizabeth's house to watch the children (they live in the same building); she takes money out of her retirement account whenever Elizabeth needs it. Her mother, whom she describes as warm and funny, is a force of nature. Sometimes this causes problems. When Elizabeth tells her mother that the family needs more private time together, her mother will back off. "But eventually Mom's back in!" That's what happens with a force of nature.

Elizabeth and her husband don't know what they would do without her mother's financial help, but the net that draws mother and daughter together is tighter than Elizabeth's husband would like. Elizabeth has mixed feelings about her mother's generosity: She is grateful, she is anxious, she feels guilty about taking from her mother's limited resources, and she wishes she were more autonomous.

A married woman in her forties with two children, Elizabeth floats into a room. She and her writer husband have been married eleven years and have a ten-year-old daughter. Until recently, they were doing fine financially, but when they adopted a second child, a little boy, the additional child-care costs proved too much—they couldn't make it without her mother's help. "Every time we are using Checking Plus [their credit line], if things are starting to build up, she hands over another five thousand dollars from the retirement fund." This help is also a way for her mother to exert control over Elizabeth and her family.

"My mother doesn't like us to use Checking Plus." I ask how come her mother knows the details of Elizabeth's checking account. She says her mother asks, and she tells.

After her parents divorced when Elizabeth was little, her mother and she became very close, so close that her mother said she would kill herself if something happened to Elizabeth. They are still entwined, something Elizabeth never has discouraged.

"We leave our front door unlocked; my mother can just come in at any time. I need my mother a lot to help out with the children, for financial reasons, and also for support." When Elizabeth is tired or feels overwhelmed by her children, she tends not to care about boundaries. When she feels better, she finds her mother irritating. Her husband resents his mother-in-law's presence but feels powerless to challenge it, and even the ten-year-old daughter is beginning to notice the intrusions. Elizabeth has started to recognize the high cost of money.

Elizabeth lives in a triangle of her own creation, caught between her mother and her husband. At some level, this suits her. She goes to her mother when she needs maternal attention and closeness, and back to her husband when she senses she is losing him. When she is closer to her husband, her mom gets tense, and when she is closer to her mother, her husband gets grumpy.

The money complicates things, because her husband feels that he can't really establish his own position in the family as long as they depend so much on his mother-in-law. He certainly can't tell her off, and he can't urge Elizabeth to, either. This triangle was set up long before the family had money problems, but her mother's generosity, coupled with her naturally anxious personality and her need for control, is making things tense.

"The hard part is how we negotiate boundaries. Sometimes they are not negotiated well and sometimes there are no boundaries at all," Elizabeth says.

Nonnie, as she is known, gets anxious when she notices that things are getting out of control in Elizabeth's frantic household. One morning, for example, she went down to the apartment, and the daughter, who is scattered, couldn't find the gloves and hat she needed before leaving at 7:30 on a ski vacation with her friends. This ordinary chaos of a busy home became a crisis for Nonnie. "We can't find Olivia's hat! How is she going to go skiing?" She got so panicked that Olivia turned to her mother and said, "Nonnie is being crazy about this hat."

Elizabeth has a terrible time dealing candidly with her mother. When Olivia complains, Elizabeth sends her to Nonnie, and when her husband complains, she sends him to Nonnie. It makes sense to her, but it doesn't really do the job. Elizabeth could set the ground rules, but she is thoroughly ambivalent.

"I so appreciate the way in which she's been so giving. But along with that comes the problem of her feeling overly invested and overly anxious about the outcomes of things."

"By trying to save me," Elizabeth says, "whether it's financially or emotionally, her behavior is not in anybody's best interest." Even though Elizabeth understands that this degree of closeness isn't good for her marriage or her children, she still feels dependent, and she is afraid that if she sets boundaries, her mother will be angry and stop helping them. Elizabeth's unlocked door symbolizes how much she needs her mother.

"Will you always leave the front door open?" I ask. She nods, admitting that she's not going to set limits. But things may not stay this way forever.

"Olivia locks the door!" There it is—the next generation.

✦

Sometimes events beyond our control put an indelible stamp on a family. In Aaron's family, the privation of his grandmother and his mother, a result of the Holocaust, cannot be overcome, even by wealth.

Enjoy

"We're a small family. Everyone was wiped out in the war.
We only have each other. Enjoy."

That is Aaron's attitude toward spending his parents'
money, a philosophy his mother only partially endorses
and one his father goes along with. With big brown eyes
and a halo of reddish hair framing an open face, Aaron is
a man of quiet humor and sweetness. These qualities con-
tribute to his magnetism. His grandmother, whom he
loves but who was cruel to his mother, survived Auschwitz.
His mother was born in 1946 in a DP camp and moved to
Israel with her parents in 1948.

After a tragic childhood, his mother came to America
as a young woman. A stunning woman in the European
style, she is strong and extremely generous. She is also
concerned about how money is spent. Aaron's father was a
terrific athlete, good enough at baseball to go into the mi-
nors after college, but his parents objected. He is a successful businessman. Aaron's sister is a natural athlete and
a gifted young filmmaker. Her parents supported her
while she was in film school, but she hates to take money
from them now. Aaron loves to, and that's where the conflict with his mother comes in.

"For instance, how much I am willing to spend for a
pair of jeans or a leather bag, or on a hotel room in Hawaii
on vacation," he explains, makes Aaron's mother nuts,
while she, in turn, makes Aaron feel terrible.

"She used to give me the guilt trip and it made me very

uncomfortable." When they go shopping together, Aaron will see a cashmere sweater marked down to eighty dollars. To him, since it used to be three hundred dollars and it's now eighty, it's a bargain.

His mother says, "How can you spend more than fifty dollars for a sweater? I don't care what it's made of."

"Mom, I really like this sweater," he replies. Then he begins to feel guilty.

"Okay, I'm not going to get it."

"No, get it if you want to. Just get it if you want to." More guilt.

"I don't feel right. I can't." They leave the store empty-handed and have a fight in the car, because he really wanted it and she made him feel so bad about it that he couldn't buy it. Aaron is devoted to his mother.

"She's my mom. She's like my best friend. I love her to death. When she goes, I'm jumping in there with her."

The family philosophy is "all for one and one for all." His mother would scrub floors with a toothbrush to pay Aaron's airfare home for the holidays. When her children come home, she cries with joy and prepares lots of food. And she always takes them shopping.

"Let's go and buy you guys something," she'll say. They have a ball. It's a very teenage-shopping-spree experience.

People who suffered privation generally go to extremes. Either they give their children everything they can afford, making up for what they missed, or, since they had nothing, they believe that their children should also overcome obstacles. Aaron's mother has wisely chosen the middle road. She would do anything to feed her family, and to educate them. Aaron knows that he can rely on his parents to help pay tuition costs for his children if he can't afford to. But when it comes to conspicuous consumption, she has a problem. It makes her a four-star bargain hunter, her daughter tells me ("Always check out the sale racks," her mother says; "you just never know"), but she objects to Aaron's attitude of entitlement. His father is the opposite.

Aaron says, "I'll take my dad's credit card and just say, 'See ya,' because I've seen his bank statements. I used to work for his company; I know what he has." One summer when Aaron was working for his father, he had some business that required him to look at the company's books. When he saw how his father spent his money, Aaron told his sister, "I have no problem with taking gifts from them, especially from Dad, who was a shitty father growing up."

Father and son never had a close relationship. Aaron says that when he was young, his father was absent and not accepting of him, and they both know it. Aaron still resents his father, and he feels that he is getting payback for the rejections of his youth.

His father tacitly accepts the fact that he messed up with his son in those formative years, and he is willing to pay the price. His mother has created a good and full life from the ashes of the Holocaust. If she takes her son on shopping sprees, that is a celebration of survival; if she shudders at his extravagance, that's her way of remembering where she came from.

Give and Take (Back)

When Diane moved home to be with her dying mother and then decided to stay in town to be near her widowed father, she wanted to buy a house. Like so many first home owners, she lost her bid for the house of her dreams. She was crushed. As she started looking again, she just couldn't find anything acceptable in her price range. At that point, her father said, "The kinds of places you are looking at are just not good investments." He generously offered to take out a second mortgage and lend her a chunk of money so that she could find something better. Her father's loan made all the difference in what she could buy, and Diane was grateful.

"We made a deal where it would be a good investment for him, because he would earn appreciation interest," she explains. She would pay him back when she sold the house. A couple of years later, interest rates were low, and her income had declined. So Diane decided to refinance.

"Dad started pushing for some of his money back," Diane says. She told him that the whole point of refinancing was to reduce her payments, not increase them, and she explained her financial problems. As usual, her father didn't really listen. He would say, "Okay, okay," and then he would start up again a week or two later, as if that discussion had never taken place. Finally, Diane said, "Dad, my need is as great as yours." He listened but heard nothing. Diane gave in. She refinanced and paid her father back the fifty thousand dollars, plus interest. Diane tells me she got the only refinancing in history where she came out paying more than she had the month before.

"It made me very resentful," she admits. But Diane can't hold grudges, so she managed to put her feelings aside. "He's a worrier in terms of money," Diane tells me. "He thinks there's never going to be enough."

This story shines a light on two sides of the money issue. The first is history: Diane's father, a son of the Depression, never made much money, and he is afraid for the future. He does not know how long his savings will last, and he wants to maintain his standard of living. This is a universal concern among members of his generation. If they saved and did well, they thought they would have plenty. But they worry. The second aspect is the relationship between father and daughter. Diane's dad was always self-involved, and his attention to his children was fleeting. His great generosity in helping Diane out with her house was undermined by his fear for his own well-being. "This is the story of my life," Diane tells me.

Strings and No Strings

Lizzie, a San Francisco artist, shared some wisdom about money. When she divorced her rich husband, she depended on alimony and child support to raise their two girls. Now the girls are grown, and he remains generous.

The elder daughter got pregnant when she was a freshman in college and refused to have an abortion. She married the father and was going to put the baby in day care so that she could work. Lizzie and her ex-husband offered to help the couple out financially so their daughter could stay home and take care of the baby. For the first year, she accepted their help with gratitude. Afterward, they continued to help her out by paying for some day care. When the baby was three, the young mom was ready for a job. Lizzie pleaded with her to take the money she was offering. She refused, saying, "Mom, I leave the house. I get dressed, put on makeup. I look like a human being. I go someplace and they say, 'Good job. Would you please do this? Thank you for doing that. What a good job.' I get to finish a project, and at the end, Mom, they give me money! How could you ask me to stay home again?"

Lizzie knew that was the end of that. "I could have given her all the money in the world, but she needed to be out."

Lizzie's younger daughter has not had an easy time, either. As a teenager, she was into drugs and lived on the street for a while. During those years, she dropped out of school regularly, forfeiting many tuition payments. Now in her thirties, she has cleaned up her act and is serious about finishing her education. She went to her father for more tuition money. Lizzie's former husband did something really smart. He said, "Because you've gone back at least half a dozen times and never stayed, we've put money out to no avail. So no, I won't pay your tuition. But when you finish, and show me your receipts and your diploma, I'll reimburse you."

That was fine. Her father gave her a genuine financial

stake in completing her education. Lizzie fronted her a little cash for the first semester. It worked. Now she is finishing up her degree and looking forward to graduate school, for which she plans to get student loans.

Lizzie and her ex-husband found a way with each daughter to help them financially without attaching emotional strings. There are times, though, when a parent's sacrifice is so great that the children seem unable ever to pay off their debt.

Sixty Red Roses

"They all have this sense that the family is Waltonesque—poor but happy. But it's just not, and it's never going to be," says the youngest daughter.

Martha, the daughter and granddaughter of highly regarded men, fell in love with her husband when she was in college. She dropped out to marry him. Children followed at an alarming pace. Less than a year after their first son was born, they had a pair of fraternal twins, and a year later their second daughter (and fourth child) came along. She was born with a cleft palate, and the surgeries to repair it put the family in debt. Martha was twenty-two years old, dirt-poor, and had four children under three years of age. Her abusive husband did not make enough money to cover their heat, electricity, and food bills.

Martha was spirited and inventive in her struggle to make a life for her children. When there wasn't money for eggs or breakfast cereal, she picked the apples from their tree in the backyard and made them individual miniature apple pies. They took meandering rides through the countryside and sang songs when they had to walk to a gas station for a dollar's worth of gas. Somehow, Martha kept her kids going, even though she was miserable.

She tells me this story to show how well behaved her children were. On the rare occasion when Martha went to the beauty parlor, the girls would sit quietly, reading their books. A stranger asked the eldest daughter how come she was so good. "I'm just loving my mama," she replied.

Thirty-five years later, that daughter describes her mother, saying, "She was our pillar. When we had no money, she still found gifts—everything you can imagine. She'd turn the simplest thing into treasure."

"It's just incredible, if you think about it. How did this woman do it?" I ask.

"Her own internal strength, her own internal fortitude. Just because the financial wherewithal was not there, just because the father figure wasn't there half the time, she was not going to let her children do without. And she's a brilliant woman."

But the atmosphere at home was not always pleasant. Rather than disciplining the children herself, Martha would wait until her husband came home, exhausted and liquored up, and would direct him to beat the child who had misbehaved. All six (two other kids were born seven years after the first four) came in for whippings, and they all saw their parents abuse each other verbally and physically. They were relieved when Martha and her husband separated and eventually divorced.

Money continued to be an issue. When the older kids were in high school, their father called all the children together and told them that he couldn't send any of them to college. They had better get themselves scholarships and loans, he said. They did. Among the six are a teacher, a doctor, a lawyer, a minister, and a couple of successful businessmen. They all put themselves through school, and they all are paying off their college and graduate school loans. They never expected their father to pay for college. It was their mother who instilled in them the desire for an education. And despite their father's outbursts and the fact that he squandered his meager salary on women and alcohol, most of the children have a pleasant relationship with this man, who has turned his life around.

What is sad is that, while they will never forget their mother's efforts to care for them, they can no longer bear the way she deals with money. When the oldest daughter was going through school, she took out very large loans to pay not only for her education but also for her mother's. Her mother never repaid a penny.

"My mother is terrible with money. Terrible. She'll go to the Big Lots and buy crap because it's on sale. Then it'll sit in the basement, while she'll complain she doesn't have any money." Martha believes that her children have an obligation to give her whatever she needs, including forgiving her debts to them. The oldest daughter is still, at the age of forty, struggling to pay off her student loans, including the money she gave Martha. The youngest daughter deals with this by not telling her mother where her finances stand. She took Martha on an all-expenses-paid trip to Italy and takes her to L.A. for her birthday every year. But she never talks about money with her mother.

The second son is adamant about refusing to give her cash. He'll help his mother around the house, and act as her handyman, but if supplies are needed, he just won't buy them. This makes Martha furious. She ignores her son's generosity and focuses only on his refusal. The children all resent her efforts to get money from them, and they all think of her as a manipulative woman. This breaks Martha's heart. She cannot see their point of view at all. She thinks their debt to her is so enormous that it can never be repaid.

Because of her financial illiteracy, Martha defaulted on student loans she took out in graduate school, which means that she can never go back to school. She is in a panic about her future. Her children, she believes, are ungrateful. When I tell her that they revere her, Martha's eyes fill with tears and she complains that they never say that to her. When she complains about the fact that her daughter the doctor refuses to give her medical advice, she shrugs off my reply that doctors don't treat family members. When she is together with her children, she says she feels like "the odd man out," because they don't pay her enough attention.

She understands what her sacrifices did for the children, but she looks back with regret at what she gave up for them. As grateful as they are, the children have found ways to distance themselves from her. They love her, but they are determined to redeem their debt on their own terms.

When Martha turned sixty, her eldest daughter—the

one she owes so much money to—suggested that each of the six children give her ten red roses, for a total of sixty. They all agreed, and they sent her ten red roses apiece. For a nanosecond, Martha felt her children had done right by her, but it didn't last. How could it? When you believe that your children owe you everything, there is no way that they can repay you.

The emotional bankbook Martha kept all those years haunts her family. But that isn't always the way money goes back and forth between the generations. Parents and grown children who have the resources and want to be generous sometimes invent ways to give that will always be remembered with joy.

Being able to show your appreciation to your children or to you parents is a great thing. Some people seize the opportunity to do this, to very good effect.

A Safe Car

Larry, forty-seven, is devoted to his parents and extremely respectful of the older generation. He venerates his father and feels deeply responsible for his mother. His parents divorced many years ago, and his father remarried and has a fourteen-year-old son. Larry has been a success, and he makes a good living. He is devoted to his wife and son. When his parents were turning seventy, he decided to give each of them a surprise gift.

He called each parent and said, "Hi, I'm taking you away for your birthday—anyplace in the world you would like to go. Just the two of us, for a week." They both objected at first, but Larry is an exceedingly effective negotiator. His father chose Warsaw (with a few days in Paris). His mother chose Italy.

"What made you decide to do this?" I asked Larry.

"Well, the monthly dinners were getting hard to sustain. I had thought we could spend real time together on a trip, and that I could show them how grateful I am for everything they have given me. I also wanted to show them that I've made it financially."

"How did the two trips go?" They were wonderful.

Recently, his mother, who lives in Maine, needed to buy a new car, and she was discussing different models with him. She could afford only a light car, but she needed one that would do well in the snow.

"What does the car cost?" Larry asked. It was about sixteen thousand dollars.

"I'll make up the difference between that model and a Toyota or a Honda, or any car that is safer." She objected, but his rationale was irresistible.

"This is for me, Mom. Remember when I was seventeen and you made me drive a good car? You said it was for your comfort and so you could have a good night's sleep. That's what I need now—not to worry about you in the winter." What finally made this offer irresistible was Larry's promise that when she no longer is able to drive (she's seventy-five), the car will go to Larry's son or to his half brother. That sealed the deal. She bought the new car and loves it.

Larry is aware of the passage of time. One day he had a talk with his seven-year-old son, a math whiz.

"How old will I be in thirty-five years?" he asked his son.

"You'll be eighty-two."

"And how old will you be?"

"I'll be forty-two, Dad."

"So when we go to the Rangers games then, will you help me up the stairs?" The little boy ran off to play. Who will take care of Larry when he is old? I put my money on Larry's son. Larry's treatment of his parents is not lost on him. Although he didn't take them both abroad and buy his mother a car to impress the boy, Larry understands the power of a good example.

The Generous Generation

My second father-in-law was a man of great energy and intelligence. Born in the second decade of the twentieth century, he was a successful physician and an enthusiast about life. He died in his late eighties, leaving two grown children and three grandchildren. At his funeral, all three grandkids spoke.

"We are the luckiest people in this room," one of them said, "because we had Henry for a grandfather." One of the stories they told about their beloved grandpa stuck with me. He had set up a little fund so that each of the three grandchildren would have a couple of thousand dollars a year at their disposal while he was still alive. It wasn't a great deal of money, but it had to be used for something they particularly wanted—camp, music lessons, tennis lessons, a new bicycle, or a set of skis. Their grandfather's generosity remains in the grandchildren's hearts decades later, and for me it sets the standard for wise giving—just enough to make a reasonable wish possible, a gift that allows each child the autonomy to make a good choice.

Larry and Henry turned money into love. Is anything better than that? The newspapers are filled with stories of wealthy families that are torn apart after the death of the patriarch. Scandal, lawsuits, and misery ensue. It's not only the very rich who are troubled by money—wealthy families make the headlines. What are we to do about this issue? Maybe we should take a chance and talk about it with the kids.

Remember when we were told we should discuss sex with our teenagers? We were supposed to tell them about love and birth control, I think. How many of us did? I didn't. I once brought sex up with my elder boy. He looked at me with contempt, said, "Oh Mother, please," and left the room. Talking about money with grown children is just as hard. They don't want to discuss that, either. It reminds them that we're going to die. I was just telling one son what age I would have to live to be in order to see my baby grandson become president. He didn't think it was funny. It made him realize that I probably won't reach the age of one hundred. I actually saw his eyes cloud up. That is another reason to avoid the subject.

So what do we do? We bite the bullet. We let the subject of money enter the conversation. Even if we don't talk directly with the kids about the specifics of what we may need and what they may get—we may want to put that off—it wouldn't hurt to be more open with them.

You can be sure that if you have more than one child, they are talking about it with one another. They are also comparing what they have already gotten from you. And they are keeping careful accounts. So a daughter who asks for money is aware of what her siblings received; and if you are supporting one child and not the others, they notice.

Take a chance with the kids and tell them what your philosophy is (first you have to know what you think, of course—not a bad thing to do). Almost everybody is confused and anxious about money. It's easier to discuss money with friends than with our kids, if we can talk about it at all. Coming to terms with our anxiety and fear about money is the first step toward removing the heavy emotional burden it carries.

Grown kids feel better if they know you're not keeping secrets from them. They may even open up a bit. This isn't easy to do, and most people don't want to or don't think they can, but if you begin to break down the wall of silence just a bit, you may learn things that you should know, and they will, too.

PART III

The Family Connection

8

HOME FOR THE HOLIDAYS

One of my favorite movie moments is the Thanksgiving dinner scene in Woody Allen's *Broadway Danny
Rose*. Danny Rose, who is a theatrical agent for the untal-
ented, invites all his clients to his hotel room for a
Thanksgiving turkey dinner, served from foil trays that
you can heat up in a toaster oven. The man with the trick
bird is there, and so is the musician who plays tunes by
rubbing his wet finger around the rims of glasses. Watching this Thanksgiving gathering of losers is touching.
Who has not felt like an outcast at the family table?

Thanksgiving, Christmas, and other major holidays are occasions for the family to replay its emotional history around a long table. Smell and taste are two of our most deeply rooted senses, so even the aromas from the kitchen take us back in time. Many parents find themselves transported to the period when the children were young; this makes them feel they are in charge again, and they may act accordingly. This same sense of time travel can make grown children touchy. They don't enjoy feeling powerless and judged again. Because of this, they can last only a few days at home before an explosion happens.

Grown children who live far away and come home only for the holidays are under special pressure. Coming home as an adult means that you have to deal with the people and the conflicts you faced growing up. It is hard not to feel like a kid again, and many people in their twenties and thirties become upset if their parents treat them like children. It's not just the smell of turkey and the sweet scent of yams that brings back the past. It takes a major effort not to fall back into the old habits.

Andrea, who is in her thirties, tells me about driving home for the holidays. The closer she gets to the town where she grew up, the younger she feels. As she pulls off the highway and heads through the village toward her old house, her neck and back muscles start tensing up. Losing the insulation of distance, she becomes vulnerable in a way that she isn't when she is hundreds of miles away. Inevitably, once she is home for more than a couple of days, there are blowups. She describes them as "stubbing my toe on old family issues." Andrea loves her parents and hates feeling this way, but she can't help it.

When she departs, she has a giant sense of relief. She breathes more easily, her shoulders head downward from her ears, and she once again feels deep love for her parents. The conversation that made her furious does not matter so much now that she has put fifty miles between herself and her mother, and by the time she has driven a hundred miles, it is forgotten. Andrea is lucky: She recognizes the family dynamic and can deal with it—at a distance.

Andrea's experience is a common one, and it can affect both generations. I learned more about this when I recently met two of my friends. These grandmothers live in apartments and were comparing notes about the horror of long visits from their children and grandchildren. The visits seem interminable, they said. The younger woman, still a beauty in her late fifties, looked exhausted. Her son, his wife, and their child had arrived on Christmas Eve, and they weren't leaving until after the first of the year.

"It's awful," she moaned.

"Why?"

"Because the parents are always around, and we can't be at ease with our grandchild."

Her friend agreed, saying, "It's terrible."

The first woman was taking long walks alone—just to get away from the tension. Even the sharp winter wind seemed preferable to being confined in a small space with her progeny.

I saw her again on New Year's, and she looked a lot happier.

"They're gone," she chirped. "They left yesterday and we've finally cleaned up their room. He's our messiest son, and it hasn't improved. They left dirty diapers in the wastebasket—didn't even throw them out."

Here's another example of old roles intruding into the present. This mother wasn't able to get the messiest son to clean up after himself when he was a kid, and she still cannot get him to be neat as an adult. She and her husband are tense with their grandchild in front of his parents, because they have not worked out their differences about child discipline. If that isn't enough of a trial, imagine what it is like in cramped quarters, over Christmas.

Family holidays are by nature stressful. Family members who are separated by great distances don't have much of an opportunity to work out their issues face-to-face between visits. And even families who live in the same town and have a good back-and-forth can get derailed on holidays, when the siblings arrive and things get complicated.

For both generations, home can be dangerous territory, because it is a breeding ground for old issues. The good news is that there is always the potential for understanding and change. But that can only happen if everybody is willing to rewrite the old scripts. Shannon's parents were not prepared to make any changes at all. Christmas has become a symbol of her family's disintegration. Shannon is furious with her parents because they refuse to treat her as an adult. Things blow up at Christmas, whether or not she is at home. For both generations, the significance of this day is enormous. Slights or misunderstandings loom larger than they do on the other 364 days of the year.

Groundhog Day

"The last month has been really horrible. My heart's broken open. All of this makes me realize how much I need the love of my parents."

Shannon is a sad but energetic young woman, who believes that she has come to an impasse with her parents. Many of the incidents that brought them to this level of misery took place at Christmas.

Shannon's mother and father are not easy people. They were both raised by parents who were clueless about how to care for children. Her mother began yelling abusive things at her daughter when Shannon was only six or seven.

"My mom would fly off the handle and yell. She did a lot of name-calling, a lot of 'stupid bitch'—type stuff." Her father, a binge drinker, was scary when he was drunk. Shannon does not focus on her childhood, but there is no question that she suffered from her parents' behavior. What concerned her most was her parents' tendency to break off family relationships—for good. They no longer have any contact with her mother's family, and her father has no family left. They lack a model that would help them stay together as a family, despite their fights. This is a serious problem for both generations.

The recent trouble started several Christmases ago. Shannon had been away at college for a couple of years but always spent this holiday at home. As she became more accustomed to her independence, it became more difficult for her to adjust to her parents' controlling behavior. One night, she came home at curfew, as required, but she stopped by her mother's bedroom to ask if she could borrow the car to go out again with her boyfriend and their friends to watch a movie. Her mother said no in the bitter tone she'd used when Shannon was a little girl. Shannon, now a college student used to being spoken to with some respect, lost her temper.

"You know what? You can't talk to me like that," she said. She leaned into the doorway and shook her fist at her mother. Her mother's bed was across the room from the door, so it surprised Shannon to hear her mother yell out to her father, "Shannon's lost it and she's trying to attack me!" Her father chased Shannon down the stairs. Her boyfriend, who was waiting in the car, heard her father's bellowing and tried to get inside the house to help.

Her father was livid. "This is my home and my property and I can do whatever the hell I want in here," he said. He slammed the door and proceeded to kick Shannon back upstairs. She went into her bedroom and shut the door. After a while, her mother came to her room. She found Shannon lying on the floor of her closet, in the fetal position. Shannon assumed that her mother was there to help. Instead, she opened the closet door and shouted,

"How dare you! You know your father has a heart condition. If he has a heart attack because of tonight, I will hold you personally responsible." Somehow Shannon got through the rest of her vacation. She went right into therapy when she got back to school. That helped, and over the next couple of years, Shannon was able to establish a more adult relationship with her mother, who began to confide in her for the first time. Things were going along pretty well until another of Shannon's Christmas visits.

This year, Shannon accompanied her father to a holiday business party one evening, because she wanted to drive him home. The minute they arrived, her drunken father began another fight with her mother. It was too much. Shannon felt she was too old to participate in the family drama.

Enough is enough, she told herself; I won't go home for Christmas next year. Even though she stayed away, Shannon could not keep from getting embroiled in another family Christmas drama. It had been a tough year. Shannon was accepted into graduate school, but because of a snafu in her paperwork, her scholarship did not go through. She asked her parents to cosign her student loan. They refused. Her father told her they couldn't help because they were buying a third house. Her mother's comment still rankles: "Serves you right. You were foolish to think you ever could have done this."

Eventually, Shannon got a friend to cosign, and she began school in the fall. By Christmas, she was deeply involved in term papers and exams. She had no money, so Shannon decided to forgo the usual gifts and festivities, but she planned to send her parents a card. Somehow, in the flurry of finals, she forgot. Shannon admits that it might have been a subconscious omission because she was so angry with them for not helping her, but she never anticipated the fallout.

On Christmas Day, not hearing from her parents, Shannon called them. She left messages at home and on their cell phones. Nobody returned her calls. Shannon was getting frantic.

Christmas Day, I'm their only child, and I'm not with them. Something must be wrong, she thought. As the long day wore on, she got frightened and called the nonemergency police in their town.

If they're in a ditch somewhere, no one is going to be looking for them; I'm the only person, she reasoned. The police did a drive-by and told her nothing looked awry. The next morning, she still had not heard from either of her parents. She again left messages on all their phones, saying, "I am really worried something's happened to you. Please call me. Please call." She tried one last thing before going to the police again: She dialed her dad on his car phone. He picked right up. In hindsight, Shannon realizes that he had answered because that was the only phone that didn't have caller ID. He just laughed when Shannon said, "Do you realize that I called the ER and the police?" The truth slowly came out.

"You know, your mom is pretty mad at you."

"Really? Why?"

"You didn't send us a Christmas card."

Silence.

"Dad, it's a card! You don't put your child through torture because they don't send you a card." Her parents had received all of Shannon's messages; they knew how frantic she was, but they were angry with her and wanted her to know it.

Shannon decided it was best to send her parents a letter, expressing her feelings clearly. "I am not doing this to punish you or to be mean, but I am so thrown by what happened this Christmas that I just need some time to think. I'll call when I'm ready, but I need a little time," she wrote.

If you have learned from your parents that breaking off relationships is the way to solve family conflicts, then asking for a time-out is an improvement. Shannon was no more adept at resolving conflict than her parents, although she was trying. It didn't work. Her mother was upset by the letter, and Shannon heard her mother's anger on her answering machine: "This is your mother. Please call me."

Shannon was still too angry to speak with her. She was worried that they would get into a more serious fight and break things off permanently. She may also have secretly enjoyed giving her mother the silent treatment. A month later, her mother sent her an E-mail, continuing her effort to elicit a response: "I just think you are a terribly selfish and immature person. By the time you were thirty and I was sixty-two, I would have thought we could have had an adult relationship. You clearly aren't capable of it. I do love you, but I am very mad at you right now."

Notice how every communication raised the stakes and

made the next interaction more dangerous. Shannon waited a few more days and then replied to her mother's E-mail with an entreaty that expressed her desire for the love and respect she so desperately wanted: "I need you to know how it felt when you treated me this way. I need you to be able to express your love for me. I need you to believe in me and support me. And I want to be able to call you when the shit hits the fan. I want my mom." She was asking them to treat her with love, but as a grown-up, not as a child whom they could control and punish. She hoped for a reconciliation.

"I don't want a phone call twenty years from now saying that you guys are on your deathbed and then I have to make my peace with you," she wrote.

Shannon's letter didn't break things off, but it didn't improve the situation.

"I can't believe how selfish you are," her father wrote back. "We clearly have spoiled you and it is now time for us to spoil each other." He obviously wanted Shannon to apologize, but along with the anger, you can hear hurt and longing in his words.

"I want you to respond to this E-mail. You have a lot to make up to your mother. I don't know how you're going to start, but you'd better think long and hard and find a solution."

All her life, Shannon had gone along with most of her parents' demands, even though she thought they were not fair. But now she needed to stand up for herself, even if it meant ending the relationship. "I am done. I am done. I can't will you to be a better human being, and I can't will you to look at what's going on. It's clear that everything I say or do seems to get twisted or turned around," she wrote.

Shannon is still too hurt to believe that they will reconnect, but she cannot give up hope—these are her parents, after all. She feels defeated by their unwillingness to treat her as an adult, but she cannot go back to being a child.

One of the hardest lessons to learn as we get older is that we cannot change the other person; we can only change ourselves. Shannon is not ready for this. She's too angry with her parents, and she sees herself as the wounded party. Even though she knows that these arguments repeat the dynamic that caused her parents to break off with the rest of their family, she has not figured out how to end the impasse.

Maybe Shannon's parents' feelings were hurt when she decided to stay at school over Christmas. Perhaps at some level they realized how much refusing to cosign her loan had hurt her feelings, and maybe they were looking for that card as a sign that she had forgiven them. Their guilt may have fueled their rage at her. People who have little understanding of their own feelings use anger to cover their hurt. Notice that they have not broken off with Shannon. That's a big deal for them, and a sign of how much they love their daughter.

The burden of reconnecting weighs heavily on Shannon's shoulders. She is right in thinking that her parents are unfair, and that it will take more than a few months to forgive such a hurt. But the intensity of their connection and her parents' determination not to break off with her bode well for the future. A series of holiday encounters crystallized the problems in Shannon's family. Let's hope that by next Christmas, both generations will take some steps to find each other again.

Rachel and Her Children

A holiday at home is like a petri dish in which all the old feelings and relationships spring to life and multiply. Peggy was surprised to see this happen one Christmas a few years back. The family was not at home, but in the village where two of Peggy's grown children and their families now live. Four generations were present at the holiday, and there were many young children. Peggy was on guard, as most grandparents are, about how the little ones would behave on this important day, since her aging mother, the matriarch, would be with them.

Peggy and her husband raised their three children in a house next door to that of her in-laws. She was very close to her mother-in-law, and the children were in and out of their grandmother's house all the time. Early in their marriage, Peggy and her husband bought and remodeled a weekend house located on the ocean, about two hours' drive away. This getaway was essential for Peggy and her husband—they needed to spend part of the week away from his parents. Soon it became a haven for the whole family. Friends came to stay and help in the renovations, and the three children brought friends along, too.

The old house on the water was important to them all. In fact, when they grew up, the two younger children, a son and a daughter, settled in a town nearby. Peggy and her husband take great pleasure in the fact that they can still spend weekends together with their grown children and their grandkids.

The two young families have become very close, largely because of Rachel, the younger daughter and middle child.

"Rachel is kind of the glue that holds the family together. She is our sunniest child, the one everybody talks to," says her mother. "She's nonjudgmental and always funny and cheery."

Peggy had no reason to expect any problems at Christmas. This year, the children offered to take the burden of Christmas dinner from Peggy's shoulders. She was delighted to turn Christmas dinner over to Rachel. Peggy was pleased at the thought of just playing with the grandchildren, instead of planning, shopping, and cooking. Like most families, they observed many traditions, and Peggy had not considered either Rachel's laissez-faire attitude or her own mother's demanding one. This amazingly strong and healthy nonagenarian thinks she is still in charge. She nags Peggy about her haircuts and phones to warn her when it's too icy to drive. Born in the first decade of the twentieth century, she is an old-fashioned woman with strong opinions and she believes that parents know best, no matter how old the children may be. Peggy's mother never approved of Rachel, who didn't give a fig about the things that matter to her grandmother. Now a mother herself, Rachel has a high tolerance for chaos and messiness.

The dinner was a disaster. Rachel has never planned ahead, and getting all the food to the table at the same time is not one of her strengths. That would require, for instance, thawing the Christmas turkey ahead of time. The meal was very late, and dishes appeared haphazardly. Grandma was not happy. The table was not set when all the guests arrived, and then in her rush, Rachel neglected to put out the matching china. Grandma was seething. Peggy tried to avoid her mother's angry looks and forced herself to smile at her children. It was excruciating. Peggy was stuck between the generations in a conflict she had not been able to resolve when Rachel was small and could not handle today. While she herself has always made Christmas dinner work perfectly, she wishes she had some of Rachel's happy-go-lucky qualities. The two young families, of course, were oblivious to this all, since they were having a great old time. But Peggy could hardly eat. She adores Rachel and never wanted to upset her mother.

After dinner, the children opened their many presents. It took forever. Rachel's Christmas was thoroughly disorganized and child-centered. By the time the last toy had been ripped from its wrapping, Grandma, hat, gloves, and coat already on, was ready to leave. She complained the whole drive home. Later, Peggy realized that if she had been thinking, she never would have let Rachel cook Christmas dinner for her grandmother. In her mother's eyes, Peggy is still the daughter responsible for making her children live up to her old-fashioned standards. Peggy loves Rachel just the way she is, but she loves her mother and remains somewhat in awe of her. Even if the old woman's view of life is irritating, Peggy knows that each Christmas could be her mother's last, so she placates her. Peggy is unhappy that she let Grandma spoil Christmas and blames herself for allowing things to get out of control.

The next year, Peggy decided to take back Christmas dinner. She didn't want to be rejecting of Rachel, who had worked so hard to entertain the whole family, so she worked out a compromise. The family spent Christmas Eve at Rachel's. The grandchildren opened all their presents in the warm, cozy atmosphere of Rachel's house, and Peggy's mother, knowing that a proper meal would be served the next day, was gracious and relaxed. She was right. Dinner came out of the oven on time, and the table was set perfectly with the proper china and crystal. Someday Peggy will be able to give Christmas back to her children. Then she will discover what kind of matriarch she really is. Meanwhile, the dynamic of the generations will continue as it has for nearly a century.

Play Ball!

Jerry and Nancy have three grown children, a daughter in her middle thirties and a pair of twin sons, who are two years younger. The family is close, and the children are deeply engaged in their own lives. One twin lives on the West Coast with his wife, the other son lives nearby, and the daughter lives hundreds of miles away. This is a family that enjoys sports: baseball, golfing, biking, running, and skiing. When the twins were young, Jerry coached Little League. An athlete in high school and college, he was eager for his sons to play, and the boys were very good at the sport, which they still love.

"I took them to Little League to sign up," says Jerry, "and since I had two, I had no choice but to coach. I coached seven teams in ten years. For most of that time, I had both boys on my team." This was a family affair. The older sister was a softball star, and Nancy was totally involved, too.

"Of all things, she developed into an expert at glove repair. She also kept score for all the games and was on duty for any injuries," Jerry says.

"One of the great things we did at dinner," says Jerry, "when they were growing up was to sit around the table talking baseball strategy." They are rabid Red Sox fans. Jerry and Nancy have season tickets, and they go to most of the home games. They would call the kids from the games on their cell phones to discuss plays and to share the excitement of winning. This family passion binds them together. It gives the parents the pretext for calling their busy children, and the Red Sox fanatics who do not live in Boston have someone with whom to share their excitement.

Sports plays an important role in many families. It is a medium through which fathers can relate to their children without having to talk much. Loving a team is also a way of loving one another. The subject of Nancy and Jerry's calls may be sports bulletins, but the undertow is affection. Talking about baseball over the phone isn't enough for Jerry and Nancy, though, who love to spend time with their kids. They are always looking for excuses to get together.

The family does not have a weekend home, but some years ago the parents discovered a lovely small inn in the mountains, on a lake. The two of them stayed there for a week and were charmed. The owners had just opened the inn a year before, and they were determined to make everything right for this nice couple. Jerry and Nancy decided it was time to start up a new family tradition: a week—or some part of it—together in the country. They called their children to invite them.

"Hey, kids, come to the Erinmore."

"What are we going to do?" asked their daughter, who was unenthusiastic. Her boyfriend is not athletic, and she was worried about putting him in an all-sports environment. The boys also were uncertain. "What happens if we don't like it?" they asked.

Still, the parents were paying, and the place sounded lovely, so they all decided to give it a try. It was a success. The relaxed rhythm of the inn and the lack of any schedule made it pleasant for everybody. You could lie around and read if you felt like it, but there was plenty for the energetic family members to do. And best of all, nobody had to organize activities or participate in scheduled events.

Two rituals have evolved. They always go out to dinner in the village, then go back to the inn for board and trivia games. The second ritual is dinner with Jerry's ninety-year-old mother and his two sisters, who live nearby. The innkeepers, who generally only serve breakfast, put on a lavish dinner for the entire family.

All three kids and their families have happily joined them at the inn for the last six years.

"We go to the same places and do the same things, and it's just nice to get together," says Jerry.

"The kids love it?" I ask.

"I think so. Yeah, they keep coming back! That is the test." Jerry and Nancy count the days until their next week at the inn. "Well, it is a lot of fun. Being around your children, there is nothing like that," Jerry adds.

Even the daughter and her boyfriend, who isn't a sports enthusiast, are taking tennis lessons to improve their chances of beating the twins next summer.

Changing the setting for get-togethers can help keep family members from slipping back into old roles. Inventing new rituals can also work.

No Exodus Needed

Janet loves Passover. For more than forty years, she has made a seder for the family. She cooks for days before the holiday and is exhausted by the time everybody sits down to the table. Reform Jews, she and her family always had what she called an "expedited seder"—in English, with just a little singing. But even that proved too much for her grown children. No sooner had they sat down than her sons, who were in their thirties, would begin their campaign to shorten the ceremony. The wives and girlfriends were polite about these comments, but they never seemed to be in quite the same rush. The negativity always bothered Janet, who hadn't minded it so much when the boys were small—all children squirm at Passover; it is almost a part of the ritual.

Janet came to resent the fact that she spent so much time and effort preparing for the occasion, only to have it hurried to completion by her ungrateful sons. She knew something had to change. Then she had a brainstorm. One night at dinner months before Passover, she brought up the subject with her family.

"I need your help," she said. "You know how hard I work to prepare for the seder, and how much the ceremony means to me. You clearly don't like it, or you wouldn't try to rush it. What can we do to make it better for us all?"

"We hate reading from the Hagaddah," one son said. The other nodded.

"Why don't we do our own ceremony?" That was an interesting idea, but Janet had a problem.

"Okay, but what about retelling the story of the Exodus?" That is the whole point of the seder.

"You tell the story. You love to do that anyway, Mom." The sons exchanged a knowing look.

"Okay, but if we do it that way, everybody has to bring something to read or a story to tell, and we'll go around the table and each of you will have a turn. How does that sound?" The boys agreed.

Passover arrived, and the family and guests came prepared. One read a poem, another a Buddhist essay, a couple who had just been in Italy read a piece about Passover in Rome, and one brought a letter about the meaning of freedom written by a man who had spent forty-three years in jail. It was the best Passover ever. Why? The grown children, treated as adults, participated as adults, not as bored and hungry children. The sons had privately calculated that this new system would cut down the ceremony time and speed up the meal. It didn't happen that way, but nobody minded, because everybody brought something of their own to the table. Now Janet saves each year's contributions and adds them to last year's pages, so the family has a spiritual and emotional record of each year. She looks forward not only to the cooking and the ceremony but also to the interesting ways in which her grown children are changing this celebration to meet their needs and interests. Next year, when the baby arrives, they will add photographs to the family Hagaddah.

Holidays can be a source of misery or joy; they also can be works in progress. We have to accept the fact that we cannot change people to suit ourselves, and the older we get, the less inclined we are to change ourselves to suit our children. But it is easy enough to try going to a different place or inventing a new ritual. Since holiday ceremonies and vacations take on a mythic role in our lives and the lives of our children, we need to pay special attention not only to the past but also to the future. Think of the new customs grandparents create with their grandchildren. Little ones are ritual makers from the beginning. They love a certain song, a special walk, a favorite food. Perhaps we can invent new rituals to take the place of old habits and reinvigorate family gatherings.

Last summer, I came across a ritual that a family had just invented. A young woman who was driving me home in a rental car told me how close she and her family are. She described a new custom they recently created. They utter these words to one another whenever they say good-bye.

"I love you."

"God bless you."

"Be safe."

If you interrupt the flow of these three sentences at any point, you have to start again. Her family invented this good-bye after her great-grandfather died. He cared tremendously about them all, but he never told anybody how much he loved them, except for the few people who were with him on his deathbed. Afterward, the family talked about his inability to express the love they knew he felt. So they decided that since life is unpredictable, they would end every conversation with these words:

"I love you."

"God bless you."

"Be safe."

Think about using these words when you say good-bye to the people you love. I know it sounds corny, but the failure to express love is a serious thing. Imagine what you might do to make holidays more meaningful for everybody. You would be surprised at how eager everybody will be to make adjustments and changes to enrich these times. They are so precious, as is every greeting and good-bye.

9

THE SONG OF LOVE

It takes a lot of work to break up a family. It's almost impossible to stop loving your parents, and even more difficult to stop loving your children. Given this obvious truth, what's the matter with us? Why can't we find a way to be easy with our grown kids, and just be close and relaxed? There are a lot of barriers. Sometimes we just don't get along with one or another of the kids or don't warm to the person he or she married. Maybe a son or daughter decided years ago to establish distance from us, for reasons we may never know. Old fights, new issues—they all have the potential to keep us apart emotionally. Perhaps we're both disappointed in one another: We are too demanding, and our disappointment in them shows; or, our old quirks still rub them the wrong way.

The families in this chapter stand out because of the determination of the parents to communicate their love, and the ability of the grown children to see their parents as people, not as symbols of authority or judgment. Members of both generations accept one another, flaws and all.

I don't know for sure what makes this happen, but I do know that a motif of deep spirituality runs through these families. It's not the specific religion they practice that helps them, but the wider perspective that all great faiths provide.

The Lollipop Kid

Tina speaks with energy, and her words come out rat-a-tat. She is about five-two, with a mop of curly brown hair framing her round face. She expresses love for all the generations of her family in detail and with fervor. Her maternal grandmother died a little over a decade ago, when Tina was twenty-nine.

"Even though I was fortunate to have known her for a long time throughout my adult life, I have never stopped thinking about all the things I wish I could still ask her," says Tina. "My grandmother started every day sitting in her chair by the window, saying her Rosary. She was old-fashioned in the best ways. She was such a kind person.

She was a great lady." Tina and her husband were very close to her.

"When we first got married," Tina continues, "we lived fifteen blocks from my grandmother. We used to keep our car in her garage, and we'd walk down the street to see her and have dinner with her."

One memory sums up their relationship. "She used to alter all our clothes for us, and she never learned how to sew on a sewing machine—she did everything by hand. She'd hem our winter coats, and I'd have three or four different try-on sessions. First she would mark, then pin, and then baste. I just hated it. But I still have this skirt that she hemmed for me when I was in high school.

"My mother is very much the combination of her own parents," says Tina. "She is very peaceful and loving and good-natured."

"Does your mother sew?" I ask.

"No, not really. But she is a good cook. And she could put on a bandage so you wouldn't need stitches. She has backbone and she knows what's right, and she will always do what's right. My mom will always do that little extra thing for somebody who needs it, and sometimes before they even know they need it."

Tina talks to her mother two or three times a day and remembers with joy the time they spent together when each of her two babies was born.

"Oh my gosh. She stayed with me for a week each time. It was perfect. It was so great. She came, and she's organized—she's got systems. She showed me everything." Her mother gave her advice in a nice way, not a bossy way.

"She helped me. She knew how to wrap the baby up in a blanket. She knew how to prop her up when I was feeding her. Whenever anything is wrong with my kids, I call her before I call the pediatrician."

Tina's father, a self-made man who never finished high school, is more literate than most. He spent his career as a PR man for Broadway shows. He is gifted with his hands and is always fixing things, making things, doing things for Tina and now for her girls.

When the family moved to a house with a big backyard, Tina's father had a vision. He built a complete western town in the yard. It was a child-size, perfectly scaled, perfectly detailed. There was a two-story hotel/saloon, a jail, and a general store. The bank and the church were just fronts. Everything was connected with wooden sidewalks. Then off in some trees was a fort with a lookout post. Her father also loved making Super-8 movies, and so he produced and directed Westerns, with the children as the stars.

"The first movie was called *The Lollipop Kid,* and it featured my little brother, who was maybe three years old at the time. My sister played his love interest, Miss Kitty. I played everyone else: the preacher, the bad guy." Her father was written up in the local newspaper as the Cecil B. DeMille of Long Island. Tina is the oldest in this upbeat family. She excelled in school and fell in love with her future husband when she was eighteen.

She had just graduated from an Ivy League university when tragedy struck her family. Her younger brother, the

Lollipop Kid, was killed by a drunk driver. This changed her family and, of course, it changed Tina.

"The day my brother died gave my life context. I had always been my parents' daughter, but I was a kid. I was twenty-two. I remember that day, finally getting home and seeing my father throw himself on the ground in the backyard. I had never seen him cry. That changed everything in my life. I suddenly realized that until I had children of my own, I was never ever going to know what my brother's death meant to them." Tina became an adult at that moment.

"I had to help them in ways I couldn't even imagine. I was going to have to do whatever I could—not to make things better, because there was no way to make things better, but to try to hold them up, to the extent that I could. If being present was all I could do, then that's what I would do."

She decided to live at home the next year, instead of living in the graduate school's dormitory. I don't think Tina appreciates the significance of that gift to her grieving parents. She shored them up during that year of sorrow. Eventually, as it inevitably does, the mourning lightened. Tina married her college sweetheart and had two delicious daughters. Tina's girls have wonderful grandparents.

"Whenever they visit, they never come without bringing food, and there's always a stack of clippings and comic strips that my father has cut and pasted into a book for my daughters."

The children see their grandparents all the time. Grandpa takes the older one to soccer practice, and their grandma is always in and out of her daughter's house. They take the girls home to their house one week during the summer for their "vacation." The girls sleep late; they get special hairdos every morning; they can eat breakfast on little tables in front of the television.

Last year, Tina's father fulfilled his dream: to take his first granddaughter to Rome. Even though he knew the city well, he hired a car and driver to take them around. They spent long afternoons at the Piazza Navona, and the grandparents insisted that the twelve-year-old have gelato twice a day. There was no tension during the trip, because they were all having such a good time.

Tina and her family carry on the traditions that began generations ago. She is a lector in the local church, and they take the girls to Mass every Sunday. Last year, when the eldest daughter started singing in the children's choir, she said, "Mommy, I see the Mass from a totally different perspective," and she meant it both ways—because of where she is standing in the choir and also because she can see everything the priest does as he celebrates Mass.

⚬

Tina comes from a tightly knit family, and she and her husband include her parents in everything. I don't know too many women in their forties who would be happy having their mom coming in and out of the house at will. Tina might have felt claustrophobic with this degree of closeness, no matter how wonderful her parents are, but she doesn't. I think that's because the death of her brother made her see her parents as people, suffering before her eyes. Tina grew up when she witnessed her father's grief, and she went from being a young girl in her twenties to a grown woman.

Tina is mindful and alert to every change in their lives. "In sickness and in health" is what they say at weddings. It's also true for families. Joy and fun give us the strength to endure tragedy, and this family shields itself with love.

All the Names

"Every night we'd kneel in the living room to pray, and finish up by saying, 'God bless Mommy, Daddy, Ronnie, Donny, Gary, Terry, Jenny, Matthew, Cindy, Randy, Billy, Steffi, Aunt Cecile, Cousin Paul, and all our relatives in France, and thank you for our blessings, and deliver us from evil. Amen.' "

This is how Matthew, a West Coast filmmaker, describes evening prayers in his home. Matthew tells me that his father's faith was a form of nurturing love for the entire family. A devout Catholic, he was influenced by, and a good friend of, Dorothy Day, the great social reformer and founder of the Catholic Worker Movement. Matthew is a Buddhist married to a Jew, and they will celebrate their daughter's bat mitzvah in a couple of years. He feels his father would approve. His father's religion, like his life, was one of inclusion and acceptance.

"I really believe that spirituality is the most important thing in a person's life. That is what my father taught me—so whatever you choose, choose something and make tolerance its cornerstone." Tolerance was essential in such a large family.

Matthew's father would come home every day at lunch and take over for his exhausted wife. She would have been a professional woman, were it not for her religion and her fertility, but she still managed to read as many as twenty books a week, which would not have been possible without her husband's help. He would come home, put an apron on, and say, "Dearest, go to the library. I'll take care of everything." After lunch, he would clean up and return to the office. Chores took up virtually all of his free time. His salary could not support the family. Matthew found letters his father had written his father, asking for a few hundred dollars each month to help make ends meet. This does not seem to have affected his good humor or love for his family.

Matthew's father was generous, even though he had little money to spare. He insisted that the children did not have to work while they were in college. It only cost sixty dollars a semester to send them, and he could afford that. He felt that studying and enjoying college was a full-time job. If they wanted to live away from home, then they had to support themselves.

Of course Matthew's father wasn't perfect. He had a terrible memory. He was always calling his children by the wrong names (with ten children and a dog, that's pretty easy—I used to confuse two sons and a cat). Matthew tells me that when his father picked him up at the airport once, he said, "Billy, how are you doing?"

"Dad, this is Matthew!"

"Yeah, yeah."

On the way home, he confided that the family doctor had discussed the possibility that he might be getting senile. He was in his sixties at this time.

"Why is that?" Matthew asked.

"Because I am so forgetful."

Matthew laughed. "You've always been forgetful." His father laughed, too. When they got home, Matthew told Billy about his father's mistake.

"Billy said that Dad had been calling him Coco—the name of a family dog that had died eight years before—so I don't feel so bad!"

Toward the end of his life, Matthew's father was thoroughly confused about his children's names, but they all shrugged this off with a smile. They knew when his words really mattered, and that was in prayer.

His father's voice had a very monotonous tone. He used to speak on the radio about Catholic workers, and it was too boring for the kids. But his voice had the power to heal. Once, when Matthew's younger brother was in an accident, all the children gathered in the old adobe house. Most of the kids had already left the Catholic church, so when his father suggested that they all say the Rosary, they groaned inwardly. But it had the intended effect.

"He started to say the Rosary. As we were listening to him pray, it was so reassuring to hear his monotonous voice and to connect through these words to his heart.

Our voices joined together in a Rosary were so reassuring that I was certain that it was working as prayer, because it was connecting us to one another, to our hearts, and to our brother. I finally understood that this is what prayer is, a connection through the voice and heart. From then on, I learned it was a connection to the heart, and that is where you do the prayers. He taught us that, and he taught by example."

Matthew describes his parents' old age.

"They were the kind of couple who would always hold hands. When they were in their seventies, my sister walked in on them making love. She said, 'Excuse me,' but they didn't hear her, of course, because they were deaf."

Matthew's father lived for ten years after his wife of fifty years died. He got deafer—and sweeter. He never stopped going to church. Even the grown children who had left the faith loved taking him to Mass. He would sleep through any sermon that was not about social action, but as the priest wound up, his eyes would pop open again.

"After Mass, he'd pay for some candles and put a buck in or whatever, light each one for whoever was in his thoughts. He'd be saying a prayer in his heart. We all loved to watch him."

As I listened to Matthew, I came to see that love and faith were united in his family. This alchemy could embrace the multiplicity of his children's beliefs and lives.

Matthew and his brothers and sisters think their father was a saint. They may be right, and certainly we can all learn from him. I think he was a thoroughly accepting man. He did have strong beliefs, which he shared with his kids, but they were ideas that fostered individuality and autonomy. To believe in a religion of generosity, of kindness, and inclusion, and to act on it seven days a week, not just on Sunday, tells children that they can be cherished for who they are. I think it matters that Matthew's father, such a strong Catholic, accepted a wide variation in his kids' beliefs.

He let himself be laughed at, and he was not authoritarian, either by temperament or because he was too busy with his brood. All children learn by example, and Matthew's father knew that and lived by it. That's a good dad.

Cool and Warm

"I believe so much that a mother's job is to prepare her children for life, and then let them go."

Judith is a tall, slender woman who carries herself like a dancer and speaks in the soft cadences of the Buddhist she is. Her posture tells all. Even when she's sitting on the couch, you can imagine the years she spent in the lotus position. Her hair is gray and styled in a natural way—neat, with no attempt at fashion. There's something basic about Judith: no frills, but much clarity. It's as if the years— sixty-seven for her—have crystallized her essence. Judith is a poet, and she speaks with great depth of feeling, but not emotion—I think this may be the effect of years of meditation. Judith lives with her retired second husband on a houseboat in northern California. Her home is spare and elegant, filled with light. As we chat, my eyes are drawn to the gently moving water I see through the big picture window. She tells me of her three grown children.

"Well, they are just wonderful. They are different from one another. They are all very bright, although my youngest, Michele, was dyslexic, so she had trouble in school, but she forged on and did well. Wendy is quite profound; I think she's quite sublime. And they all have a wonderful sense of humor."

"As do you," I tell her.

"Yes," she says with a smile, "but they all laugh at different things and make up different jokes. It all works well together. Also, I've been a single mother since they were in their early teen years. I divorced my husband when I was thirty-nine." She raised them on her own, living very simply. But there were advantages.

"I was always home, you know, and always taking care of them, and they completely understood about my writing. They let me be, and I sort of let them be." The kids pretty much ran wild while she was writing, but they knew that she was there.

"I discovered benign neglect. I mean in those days, kids could run all over." In those days, no one was afraid of kidnappers, or worse.

The family had very little money. "I think that was a good thing, too. They tell such funny stories about the awful school lunches I would make with wrinkly carrots, and they were embarrassed because I always put them in a great big shopping bag instead of in a little tiny bag."

They lived on a mountain, in a small old ramshackle shingle house.

"It was really quite wonderful. They all had happy childhoods, I would say. Of course, divorce is always difficult, and who knows how much they suffered over that. But my feeling was, It's better to be divorced than to have an unhappy home. Love is just so essential. Kids need to feel that and have an atmosphere of harmony."

Perhaps Judith has discovered the magic combination—harmony and humor. Still, nothing is simple, and no family is without problems. For example, her middle child and only son had a miserable patch. Just after his first child was born, he fell in love with another woman. He didn't know what to do. In agony, he turned to his mother. Judith remembers talking with him a good deal on the phone. He kept asking, "What shall I do?" Judith was full of empathy but had no answers.

"Being so much in love with this other woman, being unhappy in his marriage, but having a newborn baby, it was bad, very bad. But he followed his heart and it turned out right."

Did Judith, during this crisis, tell her son what she thought he should do? Her reply is a classic:

"I spent some years working for the suicide hot line, and I really learned to not give advice, to mostly listen. I'm sure I ended by giving advice, but mostly I tried to listen and let the caller work out a solution."

Eventually, her son left his unhappy marriage, and he is happily remarried and the father of two more small children. He doesn't have much time for his mom.

"Now that he has three little children, it's impossible to have a conversation with him anymore, but we still try. I just love seeing what a good husband and father he is. I do feel a loss, that I can't spend so much time with him because he's so busy. But you know, that will pass, and again, I am so proud of him for being that involved." The key words are "that will pass."

There is one thing Judith wishes she could tell him.

"Sometimes when you have a very successful child, as my son is, you may forget to tell that child that you are proud of them, because you are so busy encouraging and supporting the ones who are having problems." Judith has uncovered a truth. We spend most of our time as parents dealing with the problems of our grown children. But what about the ones who are doing fine?

Judith tells me she needs to say, "I'm so proud that you put yourself through law school. I'm so proud that you paid off your loans and that you are doing so well." This is an insight that bears remembering. We sometimes neglect the ones who are doing well, and we need to pay them some attention, too, and let them know how happy they make us.

No family is perfect, and in Judith's family, it is her youngest, the artist, who married a man with great dreams of success. A talented furniture maker, he went into business in a nearby town, and he expected that the whole family would help support his business. He wanted money from her mother and brother and volunteer time from her sister, who is a nurse. Judith's reaction to these demands is sharp and clear: "They should not be dependent on you, emotionally or financially. That's a hard thing for a mother, because, of course, you are tied to that daughter as if she were still a baby.

"They are twenty, thirty, forty, and they're adults, and they need to stand on their own. In the old days, you would probably be dead. You wouldn't be there for them to count on you. I think that's how it should be." She has a point. Only in the last century did most people live to the ages we now take for granted.

Because the family did not come through as the son-in-law had expected, he turned against them. He stopped talking to them and gave his wife a terrible choice: him or her family. Naturally, she chose her husband. The business did not take off, so the young couple went back to his country, where he was convinced that his family would offer the support his wife's family had denied them. It didn't happen, and now Judith's daughter is stuck in Europe with two small children and an angry husband who is having a difficult time. It breaks Judith's heart, but she mostly keeps it to herself. Her elder daughter tells me how hard this is for her mother. They have talked about this endlessly. They compare notes about how to communicate: "Should we say this to her?" "Don't mention that." They try to figure out how to mend the breach. Judith and her elder daughter are helping each other through a painful situation. Conflict of this severity is new to the family, and painful.

"Was he angry at your mom?" I ask the elder daughter.

"I don't really know what his feelings about my mom were. I know he had some complaints, but Mom didn't let him cut her out of the equation. When they lived here, she kept visiting them, although it was hard for her, because he was pretty rude to her." When they finally left for Europe, it was both a relief and a new source of anguish. The sister feels terrible about this.

"It was one of the worst things that have happened to our family, and probably one of the worst things for my mom also."

"How did your mother deal with it?"

"It's been really painful for her. I wanted her to go with me to Spain in September, but she wasn't ready. She's not angry, just sad. She felt like it was going to be too uncomfortable, that he was not ready for it yet." Judith understands that no matter how mindful you are, no matter what you do, things beyond your control take your grown children away from you. She struggles with this situation, but there is one consolation: Judith has this daughter.

She is in her early forties. As tall as her mom, with dark brown hair, she's more animated than her mother, and her life is a whirl of husband, children, and work. This is how she feels about her mother: "I just love her deeply. I enjoy her company. I see her as a wise person I can always go to."

There was a time when Judith knew things weren't going well with this daughter's marriage.

"When her husband was abroad, he pretty much took up with another woman. I'm sure at that time I said to my daughter, 'Drop him.' As a mother, you are just outraged by that sort of thing," Judith says.

"But they got back together and everything calmed down. In the end, it's not an ideal marriage, but I think she finds him the most interesting man she could be with, and probably loves him very much, and he her."

I asked Judith if her advice upset her daughter.

"No. I think I was supporting rather than advising, but who knows? It's a fine line."

This is a fine line that Judith doesn't cross. Her daughter tells me, "We've had troubles in our marriage, and I think Mom was probably disappointed in him, but she didn't try to turn me against him. She would never do that. She always tries to support whatever I want."

Judith was always a cool mom.

"As a teenager, I just thought she was fabulous. I didn't have any of the problems my friends were having with their mothers. I always told her everything I was doing. She says now that sometimes she was horrified, but she didn't say anything."

"She's a WASP with a poker face," I comment.

"Right, exactly. I watched what happened with my friends. Their mothers would expect something, they would lie to meet those expectations, and then the mother would find out about the lie, and this whole cycle of lies and mistrust would begin again. That didn't happen in our family. There were probably things I didn't tell her, but I didn't lie to her. I am trying to repeat that with my kids, for sure."

These days Judith is starting a new career as a painter, and mother and daughter love spending time together.

"We mostly just putter around. We'll talk; we'll go for a walk, that kind of thing. Maybe we'll do a little shopping in town. Or we might go see an art exhibit. Sometimes it is Mom's art exhibit now."

The relationship between these two is solid. Judith's Buddhist perspective helped keep her ego out of the picture. Her daughter seems to have inherited her mother's attitude toward the world, and the ease of their relationship is wonderful to behold.

These three families have been strengthened by their spiritual practice. Some use formal religion; some do not. With all her wisdom, Judith still struggles, just like the rest of us.

"As a mother, as you know, there's always going to be a crisis. My happiest moments are when all my children are okay. That's just how life is. We've all been through it ourselves. It is hard, because you are so bone of their bone, skin of their skin. You feel things so strongly, if you are truly a loving parent."

Judith puts into words how strongly we all feel about our kids. She also knows that we need to keep our heads straight when there is trouble. If there is one thing we all need, it's perspective. When my agnostic friend's daughter was traveling in an extremely dangerous country, she took to prayer, and it helped. Another friend says a best friend can keep you sane, so you don't explode at your children. I count waves. Every summer early in the morning, I look out at the ocean, and I count a hundred waves. The first ones come very slowly, and the middle ones come at just the right speed and the last few arrive too fast. By the time I finish, I am fully aware of how insignificant my problems are, and how little I matter in the universe.

Perspective not only helps us distance ourselves from the intense issues our children bring up; it also can help calm us in a crisis. When tragedy strikes, perspective flies out the window, but on a day-to-day basis, taking things as they come, and not getting exercised about the things we wish our grown children would not do, and not freaking out when they are in trouble or when they trouble us, is good for us, good for them, and also good for our relationship. It's a goal, not a necessity, but we can try, from time to time, to move an inch closer to that goal.

Epilogue:
A Hole in My Heart

We were on an airplane, returning home from our first family trip in over twenty years. My son's fiancée suggested that I end the book with this story, which started a couple of years ago with a phone call. It was my son David, asking if I would accompany him to his therapist. She liked meeting members of the family, he said, and he wanted to talk to me with her in the room.

Boy, this is twenty-first-century mothering, I thought. I really didn't want to go. Mind you, I would do anything for my children, but going to the therapist with your grown son? Of course I agreed. How could I refuse? As I left my office for the appointment, I was shaking my head with worry. What was I going to hear, and how was I going to deal with what came out?

I was burdened with guilt about my sons. People couldn't understand that I had any concerns, because both of them were very successful, and somehow their success spelled intimacy and joy to the outside world. We loved one another, of course, and there were no big conflicts or fights, but I wished we were closer. When their father and I divorced more than a decade before, and the big apartment was sold, we all went our separate ways. David was already living downtown, and Josh, my younger son, was finishing up college and was about ready to leave home. I had been lucky enough to rediscover my first love and we were together, and their father was finally living with his partner. Ten years before our divorce, my husband had told me that he was homosexual, and paradoxically we decided to stay married. It was not easy for either of us, but we loved each other, and we thought it would be better for the kids to grow up in an intact family.

What I remember about those ten years were the big events: moving from New Haven to New York, the boys' graduations, certain trips, and such. But it is still difficult for me to relive those times. It was hard for me to realize that I was not my husband's primary love and that our marriage was precarious. I felt alone. I'm an energetic person, so I filled my days with activity and thought I could deal with my life. I didn't know then that all our efforts to hide the hollowness of our marriage from the boys were not helpful to them. Things changed for me when I reached the summer of my fiftieth birthday and our twenty-fifth anniversary; I decided that I had to try for a fuller life. So we divorced.

My guilt over not being able to assure my sons family life as promised (by whom, I don't know) and my regret that I was no longer willing to sacrifice for them were overwhelming. My new husband, like so many of the people I spoke to for this book, was not particularly interested in forming a new family and parenting two grown men. They already had a father, and he wanted to spend time with me, not them.

The boys and I worked out a perfectly manageable system of holidays and occasional dinners, but the old closeness was gone. I did not know what to do. I would call, leave messages, and sometimes I would hear back. Our conversations on the phone were short and to the point. We would exchange expressions of love, and concern over problems, but there was no depth. There wasn't even any conflict. That is how things stood when I got a call from my older son to go with him to his therapist.

On the appointed day, we sat down on the therapist's couch, and I began to weep. I could hardly hear what they were saying. My tears were the tears of sorrow and regret, of guilt and pain. I didn't know how to get control of myself. David is a tall, good-looking guy with big brown eyes. They were filled with empathy, but he kept trying to get me to listen. I finally heard him.

"I love you and I feel that I am losing you," he said. I knew that he thought I was too distant, but what could I do? I had a new life, and I had sacrificed for the boys for ten years. David thought my new husband was the barrier between us. It's true that he didn't have much time for them, but he didn't keep me from them, either. I was responsible for myself. Now, in addition to the other guilt and sorrow for our past, I had to face the fact that I had turned away from my sons in order to embrace my new life. My tears came harder and faster. I looked up, and I saw a degree of warmth and respect in the eyes of the therapist that I couldn't fathom. Why was she looking at me with kindness? I was feeling awful about the one thing that I told myself I had done well in my life—raising my sons.

Then the rest of David's message emerged. He wanted me to know how important my love and support had been to him when he was little. He felt he always was off-kilter. He didn't think or behave like the other kids. He had been overweight and unpopular as a child. Something in the way I mothered him had kept him on track in those years. I have no idea what it was, but it was important to him that I know. He had brought me to his therapist to make sure I understood that, too.

When our time was up, we went out for a cup of coffee. I don't know what the waitress thought about this red-nosed mother and the tall, intense young man. It doesn't matter, but what I heard from David at the coffee shop was a litany of the things that I had done wrong in the last few years. It was terrible to hear, but I decided to take my medicine like a good child, even though it tasted awful.

The upshot of this encounter was a series of lunches. I would go downtown to his office, and we would sit and talk for an hour. I knew I had to hear all the things that he had felt and was feeling. Because we hadn't talked honestly in so many years, I heard many things I didn't want to know. Instead of taking the quick and reliable subway uptown to work, I would climb into a cab to compose myself for the rest of the workday. David's wish to stay connected, his words of gratitude to me, and his love made it possible for me to endure those lunches, which took only an hour but sometimes felt as if they lasted a whole day. Sometimes I would weep on the ride back. It got better over time, but it was rough in the beginning. I am not sure how I endured it. As things got easier, the subjects of our conversations ranged more widely. David insisted that his brother, who was invariably polite but quite distant, loved me just as much as he did, and that he, too, wanted to be closer to me.

I found that hard to believe, but I did start having lunch with Josh, as well. These lunches were less painful, because we talked mostly about his work. He is in politics, which is a major passion of mine, so I think I enjoyed the conversations more than he did. Josh was by then married and extremely busy. An hour had to be wrenched out of his day. Then somebody suggested that I steer the conversation away from his work, to more personal subjects. We talked about family, and children, and other nonprofessional subjects. I missed our talks about politics, but it was worth it.

We became much closer when he became a father, because I really knew how to be a grandmother and give emotional support to the new parents. I fell totally in love with the baby, which is about the easiest thing a human can do, and we started spending time together regularly.

I still felt that I had some things to tell Josh. His father and I got divorced during Josh's junior year in college. He stayed on campus that summer and didn't come home until he graduated. He moved in with me, and I was not at all welcoming. I had dinner with my new husband at the time that suited us, which was early for Josh—he came home later. He generally ordered in and ate in his room. Sometimes he joined us, but rarely. He never complained, but things were tense. When he decided to move out, I was relieved. I felt horrible about this then, and I still do. It weighs on my heart. I needed to apologize and to tell him how bad I felt.

Last summer, I screwed up my courage, and we made a lunch date. I reserved a quiet table in a restaurant near his office, and I confessed to him my sorrow at being such a lousy mother during those years, and for not being there for him. I watched his face carefully. He listened and then paused.

"Mom, do you want the good news or the bad news?"

"I think I'll take the good news first."

"It didn't bother me much at all."

"Okay. What's the bad news, then?"

"I felt I lost you long before then, so I didn't expect much from you by then. I couldn't be disappointed. I realize now that you were in terrible pain, and so was Dad. You did your best, but for me, the family just went away."

Here it was, the impact of all our planning and thinking: We had kept this secret from our children for ten long years, during which time Josh had sensed a hole in the family. He went on to tell me how sad and lonely he had been, especially when we left New Haven, and how deeply he felt the loss of what we'd once had.

"I'm very sensitive to people, you know, and I could tell something was missing," he said. I knew as I listened to him that he was right. Now I had to face the strong possibility that I had been wrong to insist that we keep our secret from the boys. I thought that we had made the right decision to hold the marriage together, and nobody knows what would have happened had we not done so in 1979. I couldn't imagine telling boys of nine and thirteen that they had a gay father. Still, I had inflicted pain on my son. I apologized, and he nodded. He was not angry anymore, he told me. None of what happened was anybody's fault. Back in a cab, weeping, I headed home.

A few weeks later, we got together again.

"So what have you been thinking?" I asked. Josh wanted to know if what he'd told me had brought back any of the sadness of those years. In fact, listening to him had made me remember a kind of gloom I had tried so hard to ignore. For the first time in years, I experienced the heaviness of our lives back then, and the effort it took me to get through the day. I told him and said that for the first time I realized that maybe we had been wrong to protect him and David from the truth. I promised Josh that I would be there for his son in ways I had not been for him.

He said, "You already are."

That was the beginning of our reconciliation.

"Where should we go from here?" I asked.

"Remember when I was a kid how close we were?"

I remembered. We would sit on the big bed and talk for hours. He and I are so alike, it was a joy to be with him.

"How about we try to get there again."

"You mean go sit on the big bed and start talking, like we used to?" I said. I was holding back the tears, and again I told him how bad I felt for all my mistakes.

"Mom, we have all suffered enough. Let's stop beating ourselves up."

As I walked down Crosby Street to the subway that summer afternoon, I couldn't tell if my eyes were filled with tears of sorrow or joy. Then I felt a rush of warmth coursing through my body. It was that love you feel for a small boy, a son.

〜

Just about that time, David suggested that we take a family vacation. We had never been together with their wives and Josh and Cathie's baby. It was a risky idea for a family that had not spent more that a couple of hours together in decades. But the idea was irresistible. I made the plans, and as the time neared, my excitement mounted, and so did my anxiety. I worried about everything. Would we get on one another's nerves? What if I overwhelmed them with my energy and love for the baby? How would the two couples get along? Would the place be nice enough? I kept calling the boys to lower their expectations, and they found my warnings amusing.

Well, it worked. We realized that just twenty-one years

ago, we had taken our last family vacation on the same island, just a couple of hotels down the beach. I remembered that trip. It had been nice, but I'd felt sad. Their father and I had sat next to each other on the beach, trying to make sure that things were okay between us.

There was no sadness now. We joked, and they played, and I got to take my grandson to the shore and hold his hands as little waves washed over his toes. It was my dream come true, and it didn't bother me that he didn't like the water at all. I felt whole again. I had my family back, and I knew that it would take a cataclysm to lose them again. I know that we will encounter other trouble and pain, and I know that life deals unexpected blows. But I feel the strong connective tissue in our family; it will get us through.

I started writing this book because there was a hole in my heart. I loved and missed my children, even though they were never far from me. I learned from the wonderful people who shared their lives with me that families come in many shapes and varieties. I learned to trust the notion that our children, no matter how distant they seem, still love us. I discovered that there is no necessity for a final rift in a family. I found people who had gone to extraordinary lengths to reconnect with their children, and I found children who were patient and compassionate with their parents.

The family is the basic unit of humankind. It's like an

atom—add different ones together and you get a new element. You can smash a family, just as you can smash an atom, but the basic energy will pull it back together, in some form or another. What keeps an atom together, and allows it to form a molecule with other atoms, is energy. What makes a family keep spinning is love.

Acknowledgments

In my years as an editor, I have always savored the task of helping my writers tell their stories or describe their theories in an exciting way. When I undertook this book, many of them came to my aid, and I am immensely grateful. I want to thank Roger Rosenblatt for telling me I had to start writing, Buzzy Bissinger for making me put my research on 3 × 5 cards, Melissa Faye Greene for giving me trust in the transcripts of my interviews, Alida Brill for her helpful first reading of an early draft, and Katherine Eban for guidance through the thickets of organizing research. I am especially indebted to Mary Pipher for her readings of the manuscript and her help and her encouragement all along the way, and to Rachel Simmons, whose insightful editing I will always treasure.

My publishing colleagues have also been extremely generous: Gail Ross and Susan Ginsburg gave me invaluable advice; Nancy Miller's friendship and enthusiasm have been wonderful; Liz Perle's encouragement was a great boost when I needed it; and Jennifer Gilmore gave me the correct title of this book (I rushed into her office all excited and said I was going to write a book called "Walking on Eggs"; she smiled and spoke). Jenna Johnson has been my helper and advisor at every step. Geneviève van de Merghel is a wonderful transcriber and smart reader of interviews, and Molly Raymond is an ace researcher. My friends Naomi Meyer and Tina Weiner have listened to me for more hours than they should care to count—thank you.

I want to thank experts who offered their wisdom and perspective: Ellen Dolgin, Roberta Sorvino, and Carol Tavris.

I especially want to thank the people who shared their lives and their stories. I have kept your identities secret, but I have tried to communicate your truths.

My old friend Phyllis Grann is the best editor on the planet; her ear and her eye are superb. Karyn Marcus, a new friend, has offered sound advice and help at every turn.

My kids, David, Josh, Cathie, and Jen, have been amazing during this whole time, and my husband, Jonathan Dolger, has been first reader, and last, the ultimate helper and advisor.

Thank you.